Business
Leadership

Viv Shackleton

THOMSON

Australia • Canada • Mexico • Singapore • Spain • United Kingdom • United States

THOMSON ™

Business Leadership

British Library Cataloguing-in-Publication Data
A catalogue record for this book is available from the British Library

ISBN 1-86152-975-9

First published 1995 by Routledge
Simultaneously published in the USA and Canada by Routledge
Reprinted 2003 by Thomson Learning

Typeset by Laserscript Limited, Mitcham, Surrey
Printed digitally in the UK by Image Archive

Learning Resources Centre

— *Contents*

—— *Figures*

— *Boxes*

—— *Tables*

— *Series editor's preface*

The rapid, far-reaching, and continuing changes of recent years have brought about a situation where understanding the psychology of individuals and teams is of prime importance in work settings. Organizational structures have shifted radically to the point where individual managers and professionals have far greater autonomy, responsibility and accountability. Organizations seek to reduce central control and to 'empower' individual employees. Those employees combine in teams that are frequently cross-functional and project-based rather than hierarchical in their construction. The traditional notion of careers is changing; increasingly, the expectation is that an individual's career is less likely to be within a single organization, which has implications for how organizations will command loyalty and commitment in the future. The full impact of the information technology revolution is finally being felt, with all the consequences this has for the nature of work and the reactions of those doing it.

The capacity of people to cope with the scale and speed of these changes has become a major issue, and the literature on work stress bears testimony to this. The belief in the importance of individuals' cognitive abilities and personality make-up in determining what they achieve and how they can contribute to team work has been demonstrated in the explosive growth in organizations' use of psychometric tests and related procedures. Perhaps more than ever before, analysing and understanding the experience of work from a psychological perspective is necessary to achieve the twin goals of effective performance and quality of working life. Unfortunately, it is the latter of these that all too often seems to be overlooked in the concern to create competitive, performance-driven, or customer-focused cultures within companies.

It is no coincidence that the rise in the study of business ethics and increasing concern over issues of fairness paralleled many of the organizational changes of the 1980s and 1990s. Ultimately, an imbalance between the aims and needs of the employees and the aims and needs of the organization is self-defeating. One of the widely recognized needs for the years ahead is for a greater emphasis on innovation rather than on simply reacting to pressures, yet psychological research and theory indicate that innovation is much more likely to take place where individuals feel secure enough to take the risks involved, and where organizational reward systems encourage experimentation and exploration – which they have signally failed to do in the last decade. Seeking to help organizations realize the potential of their workforce in a mutually enhancing way is the business challenge psychology has to meet.

The aim of the *Essential Business Psychology* series is to interpret and explain people's work behaviour in the context of a continually evolving pattern of change, and to do so from the perspective of occupational and organizational psychology. The books draw together academic research and practitioner experience, relying on empirical studies, practical examples, and case studies to communicate their ideas. Hopefully, the reader will find that they provide a succinct summary of accumulated knowledge and how it can be applied. The themes of some of the books cover traditional areas of occupational psychology, while others will focus on topics that cut across some of these boundaries, tackling subjects that are of growing interest and prominence. The intended readership of the series is quite broad; whilst they are most directly relevant for practitioners, consultants, and students in HR and occupational psychology, much of what they deal with is increasingly the concern of managers and students of management more generally. Although the books share a common aim and series heading, they have not been forced into a rigid stylistic format. In keeping with the times, the authors have had a good deal of autonomy in deciding how to organize and present their work. I think all of them have done an excellent job; I hope you think so too.

Clive Fletcher

—— *Introduction*

When I sat down to write *Business Leadership*, which is part of a series on business psychology, it seemed to me that there were at least two ways of looking at the subject. I could either write principally about what psychology has to say about leadership, or a book about how businesses are led. But they would be two very different books. The problem is that much of what psychologists have to say about business leadership is either irrelevant to practising managers and business leaders, or is ignored by them. On the other hand, much has been written about business leadership but it is not what professional psychologists would recognize as psychology. Biographies and autobiographies of successful leaders such as John Harvey-Jones, the former Chairman of ICI, or Bill Gates, Chairman of Microsoft, appear all the time. Even more numerous are books telling the reader how to succeed in business. Both categories sell extremely well, I suspect. They are entertaining, offer simple formulae for success, or both. The most striking example of how keen people are to read guides purporting to tell the ambitious how to climb the greasy pole of business success is the 1993 TV advertising campaign for Virgin Atlantic Airways. Richard Branson, the charismatic founder and self-publicist, was shown on a TV advert reading a book entitled *How to Get Ahead in Business*. In fact, the book didn't exist. It was in Branson's hands merely for dramatic effect and because the campaign was launched under the same title. Yet bookshops were inundated with requests for the book. So struck was Branson by the demand for the non-existent guide that he decided to write one. Or rather, being the successful manager that he is, delegate the job to the academic, Professor Tom Cannon.

Books recounting stories of success tend to be either too general or too specific. They either give grand prescriptions which are no help to you or me, such as 'take risks' or 'be single minded' or they are such individual stories of triumphs that they are very difficult to apply to the unique situation we all find ourselves in.

Psychology, on the other hand, strives to apply the rules and methods of science to the acquisition of knowledge about human behaviour. In occupational psychology this human behaviour is behaviour at work. So someone making a statement such as 'take risks' is challenged to define terms, explain the conditions under which the rule applies, predict consequences and provide evidence that the rule works under these conditions. It might not make such entertaining reading when the 'ifs' and 'buts' are included, but the theories or models of behaviour can at least be shown to be true or not true (that is, supported or not supported by data) when subjected to rigorous testing.

So, as a psychologist, in the end it was no real struggle to decide to focus this book on the application of psychological knowledge to leadership. What I have concentrated on, though, is that body of knowledge which is relevant to business leadership. So I have largely excluded studies of leadership of boys' camps, for example, or laboratory studies of students pretending to be leaders, which may or may not apply in the practical world of commerce, industry and the professions.

Yet this still leaves a problem. Much of what is happening that is new and exciting in the management of businesses, charities and the public sector is not yet being investigated by psychologists. If I only wrote about what psychologists had investigated, the book would have a very dated feel even before it appeared on the bookshelves. So I have included some case studies and descriptions of what is happening in the world of work.

There are many possible reasons for this gap between the writings of work psychologists and what is happening on the ground. One reason may be that psychologists are, quite simply, behind the times. This explanation may feed some people's prejudices, but it is not one I subscribe to. Another more probable reason is that the world is changing so fast that the careful, painstaking, piece-by-piece investigations undertaken by social scientists inevitably move more slowly than changes in the world of business. In addition, much of what is happening is not easily investigated by scientific methods. Take the example of 'delayering', that ugly word meaning the removal of whole tiers of management in large organizations to reduce man-power, cut costs and increase the speed of decision-making and communication flow. Psychologists and others can investigate the consequences of delayering by looking at workloads, stress levels, job satisfaction, job attitudes, and so on. But it is difficult, if not impossible, to look at whether organizations are right to delayer. We cannot collect a sample of 20 or 40 'downsizing' or 'delayering' companies, and an equal number of similar organizations that are keeping the manpower the same, as a control group, and then five years later see which are still in business, or are more profitable, or have extended their market share, or whatever other measure of success we decide upon. Life won't stand still long enough for us to do that.

So while this book concentrates on psychologists' contributions to leadership, it will also briefly discuss topics which are too recent, or maybe too difficult at the moment, to investigate properly, but where, without them, the book would not represent current thinking in business.

— Acknowledgements

There are a number of people who helped with the writing of this book.

George Davies of Cambridge Management Centres discussed ideas about derailment and kindly provided me with source material. Elizabeth Braiden of Ashridge Consulting Group has a fund of thoughts and experience of empowerment and wrote the first draft of that chapter. My wife, Margaret, drafted the chapter on women leaders. More than this, she was, as ever, patient with my impatience as I spent innumerable days researching and writing. Finally, and most importantly, my colleague Peter Wale. He researched current material and drafted four of the chapters. His energy, commitment and enthusiasm for the task never faltered, which encouraged me to keep at it as other pressures on my time crowded in.

This book is the fruit of teamwork and generosity. My thanks to you all.

Viv Shackleton

1 *Leaders and managers*

WHAT IS LEADERSHIP?

The first thing that springs to most people's minds when the word 'leadership' is mentioned is not business leaders but political leaders. Ask someone in the street to name three leaders and they are likely to cite illustrious or notorious names such as Churchill, Hitler, Chairman Mao, Kennedy, Joan of Arc, Napoleon, Thatcher or Genghis Khan. The passage in Box 1.1 shows that the fate of armies and nations can be conjured up by the simple word, but romantic

BOX 1.1 THE IMPORTANCE OF LEADERSHIP

The quality of leadership is one of the most important factors in determining the success and survival of groups and organizations. And although technology plays an overriding part under some conditions, effective leadership has oftentimes compensated for lack of equipment and resources. It enabled Henry the Fifth and his disease-ridden, hungry army of 15,000 to win a stunning victory over the French army of 45,000 men at Agincourt. It enabled George Washington to defeat the well-trained and better equipped English forces, and it enabled Robert E. Lee's troops to stand off the superior forces of the Union for over four years.

From: F.E. Fiedler and J.E. Garcia, *New Approaches to Effective Leadership*, New York, Wiley, 1987, page 1.

notion, of 'leadership'. The leaders tend to be at the top or the head of countries or armies. So, too, with business leaders, who we tend to think of as the top persons in organizations. Many have argued, though, that business leaders can be at all levels in an organization, not just at the top. What matters is an approach and a state of mind. To be classed as a successful leader by those around you in the organization you need to exercise more than managerial skills. You need leadership skills as well.

Yet this is a fairly modern view. In the past leadership has been viewed variously as a collection of innate traits, or as a question of style, or as affected mostly by the situation the leader is in. Psychologists and others have viewed the question 'What is leadership?' very differently over the recent past.

DEFINITION OF LEADERSHIP

Most definitions of leadership involve three components: influence, group and goal. First, leaders are individuals who *influence* the behaviour of others. These others are usually referred to as subordinates or followers. Second, leadership is usually examined in the context of a *group*, especially work groups such as managers and their teams or foremen and their subordinates. Third, research on leadership stresses a group *goal* that has to be accomplished. So a definition is:

> leadership is the process in which an individual influences other group members towards the attainment of group or organizational goals.

Note that the influence can be exercised in a variety of ways. It may be the 'bridge to engine room' approach, where the leader commands and controls (see Box 1.2). Or the influence can be exercised more by guiding and facilitating the group's behaviour so that the goal is accomplished. The notion of *reciprocity* is also part of many definitions. Influencing is often two way. Leaders may influence followers, but followers influence leaders to lead in one way rather than another. An influencing style appropriate for checkout assistants in a supermarket may be different from that appropriate for rocket scientists. The choices open to the leader of how to influence is one of the key aspects investigated by leadership researchers, as we will see later (see Chapter 3). Much work has been done describing the

BOX 1.2 FROM COMMAND TO COACH

> Chris Conway, the managing director of Digital, the inform-
> ation technology company, thinks that leadership and manage-
> ment has changed dramatically in Britain in the last few years.
>
> The real legacy of the recession will be the marrying of
> business, people and technology.
>
> It has called for a new style of management, one very
> different from that used in the traditional hierarchical
> organisation. The 'bridge to engine room' management
> approach will not work for the empowered, IT-oriented
> teams of today and the next century. Instead the modern
> manager's role is closer to that of an experienced team
> coach: somebody who demands a disciplined 100% team
> effort, yet who also knows how to talent-scout and
> motivate individual initiative and imagination.
>
> *Source:* Chris Conway, managing director of Digital Equipment Company, in
> an article entitled 'The Customer Comes First', *Sunday Times*, 17 October
> 1993.

choices or styles, looking at what determines the choices, and asking
whether one style or another is more effective.

Another important aspect of leadership is that the right to lead is
often *voluntarily conferred* on the leader by some or all members of
the group. In a university business school, for example, the dean is
often elected by the academic members of staff. They vote the leader
powers to influence them and the running of the school. Your local
or national politician is conferred a leadership position in the same
way, and Members of Parliament in the Conservative Party in Britain
confer the position of leader on one of its members. On a less formal
basis, leadership is conferred by groups at many different times and
places. A group of friends may recognize one of their group as the
leader, in the sense that she influences the group more than any of the
other members. There also may be informal leaders. While the
nominal head of a department may have the formal leadership
position, the real leadership may be exercised by someone lower
down the hierarchy who influences the group towards goals that may

not be those that the organization wishes to be pursue.

Finally, leadership implies that a leader *motivates* the group to spend energy in attaining the goals of the group. Influence without change or movement isn't influence. Leaders make change happen, a difficult but vitally important task. As Machiavelli warned Lorenzo de Medici back in 1514, 'there is nothing more difficult ... than to take the lead in the introduction of a new order of things'.

LEADERS AND MANAGERS

Although it is common to use the terms 'leader' and 'manager' interchangeably, nowadays many writers point to a difference between the two.

The difference is that to function as a leader, a person must exercise influence over another person in the attainment of organizational goals, as described in the definition above. Managerial functions of organizing, planning, scheduling, processing information, communicating, and so on, do not necessarily involve leadership. Some managers perform both types of function and can be described as leaders, but others do not. There is no automatic link between the two concepts. Note, too, that leaders are not necessarily just at the top of organizations. Influence can be exerted in most job functions and at all levels of seniority or hierarchy.

The distinction between managers and leaders was developed by Bennis and Nanus (1985) in their influential book *Leaders*. In it they put forward the view that:

- Leadership is path finding.
- Management is path following.
- Management is about doing things right.
- Leadership is about doing the right things.

What they meant by this is that leadership is about having a vision. It involves having a strategy or thinking strategically; it means having a view of where the organization should go or be or do; it means deciding what is important for the success of the organization; it involves envisaging the future. A leader's responsibility is to think what are the key criteria for success of his or her part of the business, and not just now but for the future.

Managers, on the other hand, are more concerned with implementing others' strategies and plans. They are concerned with running their part of the organization, making sure that the accounts get prepared, that invoices are sent out, that the service is sold, that the traffic is directed, that the research paper is written, or whatever the task that needs to be done.

A very similar view is put forward by Kotter (1990). He argues that management is concerned with activities which are designed to produce 'consistency and order', whereas leadership is concerned with 'constructive or adaptive change'. Kotter says there are four major ways that management and leadership differ:

1   *Planning and budgeting versus establishing direction.* Management involves making detailed steps and timetables for achieving results, then marshalling resources to make it happen. Leadership means developing a vision of the future and strategies for achieving that vision.

2   *Organizing and staffing versus aligning people.* Management comprises the allocation of tasks in line with plans, staffing them appropriately, delegating responsibility and monitoring implementation. Leadership involves communicating the vision so that others understand and agree with it.

3   *Controlling and problem-solving versus motivating and inspiring.* Management involves monitoring results of a plan, identifying problems with the plan and then solving them. Leadership involves 'energizing people' towards the vision. It means appealing to their needs and values so that they overcome barriers to change.

4   *Outcomes: predictability and order, or change.* Management produces predictability and order so that others, such as customers or shareholders can rely on consistent results. Leadership produces change that is often a quantum leap, such as new products or new approaches to managing people, that makes the organization more competitive.

SUMMARY

Leadership then is not necessarily just about possessing certain traits or using a particular style, although these are sometimes important. It is more about recognizing a goal and being able to influence and motivate a group towards attaining it. Leaders don't have to be at the top of the tree. They can be at lower levels in an organization. Nor is leadership and management necessarily the same thing. While early work made no obvious distinction between leaders and managers, later work points out that true leadership is about visioning and being strategic, management being more about implementing others' strategies. Earlier work was much more concerned with traits, those qualities and characteristics that were thought to distinguish leaders from followers. It is to that approach to leadership that we now turn.

2 *The trait approach*

EARLY WORK

The story of psychologists' study of leadership begins with the trait approach, sometimes called the great man/great woman theory. This approach seeks to examine the traits or characteristics which distinguish leaders from non-leaders. More recently, it has sought to distinguish effective leaders from less effective leaders, reflecting a more practical contribution to studies of organizations.

It is not surprising that traits were the dominant concern of early leadership research. For centuries, leadership positions were conferred by virtue of birth and blood. Divisions of society were 'God's will'. It was divinely ordained that the aristocracy should govern and the lower orders should toil on the farms. The ruling classes passed on their positions of power and influence in the army, the Church and commerce from generation to generation. Because the wealthy and powerful were better fed, clothed and housed, they were generally healthier, stronger and taller than the peasants in the fields or, later, the labourers in the factories. Because they could afford education, they appeared cleverer. All this meant that there was, indeed, an association between some individual characteristics and positions of leadership.

Nor is this feudal tradition completely a matter of history. Family businesses in Britain, as well as in many other parts of the world, may still find positions for members of the family which would be unobtainable at those wages, with those skills and experience, and with those favourable terms and conditions, to non-family members.

So the search for the personality traits which distinguished leaders from followers seemed logical when it was believed that leaders were

7

a breed apart. It really seemed that people were born to lead.

Yet research up to 1950 failed to yield a consistent picture of the traits possessed by leaders. A few consistencies did appear, especially that leaders were slightly taller and more intelligent than followers (Stogdill, 1974), but such limited findings were a small return for so much research. It is interesting to note, though, that the results can be explained by the more advantageous backgrounds of the leaders, referred to above. Research into the traits of leaders therefore slowed considerably after the 1950s. The accepted wisdom was that there was no evidence that leaders differed from followers in personality traits. This was explained by the fact that in modern society people can be leaders on some occasions and followers on many others. You may be chairing a meeting at one part of the day and an ordinary member at another; you might be organizing a club outing or a group of friends one day and being a follower another. If everyone is both leader and follower, it seems nonsensical to expect personality differences in the two roles. Turning to effectiveness, you might be an effective leader with one group and much less effective with another. Much depends on the nature of the task and the characteristics of followers. You could be an excellent leader of the darts team, but much less so when leading a group in a charity event. So why look for traits associated with effective leadership when the same person can be both effective and ineffective in the role?

RECENT WORK

For nearly 30 years after 1950, research concerning the trait approach went on the back-burner. It gave way to research on leadership styles and behaviour, which we will come on to later. More recently, though, the pessimism surrounding this approach has begun to dispel somewhat. House and Baetz (1979) pointed out that much of the earlier work had involved children's groups. Work with adults in work organizations had yielded rather more positive and consistent results. They agreed with the earlier conclusions that different situations require different leadership traits and behaviours, but maintained that the very nature of leadership means that the traits of sociability, need for power and need for achievement must be important (see Chapter 6).

Empirical work supports that view. Lord *et al.* (1986) conducted a meta-analysis of work published prior to 1959. Meta-analysis is a method of pooling the results of a large number of separate research studies. It allows you to estimate the impact of variables based on sample sizes of thousands, not the 50 or 70 of a typical individual study. This analysis by Lord *et al.* revealed stronger evidence than previously imagined that six traits distinguish leaders from others. They concluded that leaders tend to be more intelligent, extrovert, dominant, masculine, conservative and better adjusted than non-leaders. Similarly, Kirkpatrick and Locke (1991) have reviewed evidence which puts the trait approach in a more positive light. They suggest that the following traits distinguish leaders from non-leaders:

- drive (achievement, ambition, energy, tenacity, initiative);
- leadership motivation (personalized or socialized);
- honesty and integrity;
- self-confidence (including emotional stability);
- cognitive ability (the ability to marshal and interpret a wide variety of information);
- knowledge of the business.

They point out, though, that there is much more to being an effective leader than merely possessing a list of traits. While the traits may provide people with the potential for leadership, it is the capacity to create a vision and implement it that turns the potential into reality.

Strong leadership motivation may sound an obvious trait for a leader. After all, only those who want the weighty responsibilities and gruelling pressures of leadership are likely to strive for it. McClelland (1985) distinguishes between two types of power motivation. On the one hand, leaders may be interested in *personalized power*, which describes the motivation of leaders who seek power for its own sake, who wish to dominate others and are often concerned with the status and trappings of power. The late Robert Maxwell, former owner of the Mirror Group, allegedly displayed such traits. On the other hand, leaders who show *socialized power* motivation are more interested in cooperating with others to achieve desired goals. They work with others rather than attempting to dominate or control them. From the point of view of subordinates and the organization as a whole, the leader motivated by socialized power is obviously preferable.

On the question of cognitive ability, leaders must be able to gather,

integrate and interpret large amounts of information. Many researchers have pointed out that it is not necessary to be brilliant, though.
Leadership effectiveness is helped by above average intelligence, not
genius. Of Kirkpatrick and Locke's six characteristics, some would
argue that drive and persistence are much more important than
intelligence (see Box 2.1).

BOX 2.1 PERSISTENCE WINS EVERY TIME

Ray Kroc, the founder of McDonald's Corporation, posted this
message on his wall:

Nothing in the world can take the place of persistence.
Talent will not; nothing is more common than unsuccessful men
with great talent.
Genius will not; unrewarded genius is almost a proverb.
Education will not; the world is full of educated derelicts.
Persistence, determination alone are omnipotent.

Source: Quoted in Bennis and Nanus (1985).

In conclusion, the trait approach has undergone a revival. Recent
research suggests that traits do matter. Yet the research shows that
there are only a handful of traits which distinguish leaders from
others, and a clear distinction between effective and ineffective
leaders has not yet emerged. It is easy to get carried away. When I
run seminars for senior managers I often start by getting them to
generate a list of descriptions of effective leaders they know
personally. In a seminar of 20 people, the combined list can easily run
to over a hundred different adjectives. The research cited above
shows that most of these are not generalizable to the majority of
leaders. They merely describe the individual characteristics experienced by different members of the group which make up the seminar.
Yet traits do matter and research in psychology is beginning to show
which ones are the most important.

LEADERSHIP STYLE

After the 1950s, research on leadership began to turn to what leaders did rather than what they were. It concentrated on leadership style or leader behaviour, with the two terms used interchangeably. The trait approach assumed relatively stable characteristics, with the underlying implication that you could and should select leaders who possessed those traits. The style approach was more concerned with describing behaviour. The implicit assumption was that effective leader behaviours could be trained. You could learn to be an effective leader. Both approaches had in common the presumption that there was one best way to become a leader.

A highly influential early study was conducted at Ohio State University in the USA. The research was conducted mainly on military leaders and involved giving out questionnaires to their subordinates. The questionnaires asked about how often the leader engaged in certain kinds of behaviour, such as criticizing poor work, helping subordinates with personal problems or being willing to accept suggestions. Using factor analysis, an original nine types of behaviour were reduced down to four factors or dimensions. These were:

- consideration;
- initiating structure;
- production emphasis;
- sensitivity.

The two clusters of *consideration* and *initiating structure* each deal with different behaviours and together accounted for more than 80 per cent of the variation in subordinates' evaluations of their leaders. The two dimensions have since been found to describe leader behaviours in many subsequent studies involving many different work situations, though often called by different names. Consideration has been called relationships orientation, relation-skilled, supportive, employee-centred or group maintenance oriented. Initiation of structure has been called task orientation, administratively skilled, work oriented, production centred, or goal achiever.

The two terms can be defined as follows:

1   *Consideration.* The extent to which the leader and subordinates have a relationship built on mutual trust and liking, respect for

ideas, consideration of feelings and warmth between each other. There is likely to be camaraderie, rapport and two-way communication between them.

2   *Initiating structure*. The extent to which the leader defines and structures his or her own work and the work of subordinates towards the attainment of a goal. Structuring leaders are those who provide clear-cut definitions of role responsibility and play an active role in directing group activities through planning, communicating information, scheduling, criticizing, or trying out new ideas.

An important finding from the Ohio State work is that the two dimensions are independent. So leaders may be high on both dimensions, low on both, moderate on one and high on another, and so on. Where a leader *should* be is a different question.

At the same time, research was also going on at another American university, Michigan. The Ohio and Michigan studies were largely independent of each other. While the Ohio studies were interested in understanding the principles of leadership by asking subordinates to describe their boss's style, the Michigan ones concentrated on looking for differences in behaviour between effective and ineffective leaders. They discovered that effective leaders were employee-centred (concerned about their subordinates) whereas ineffective ones were job-centred (only concerned with the task). So despite the different and independent approaches of the Ohio and Michigan teams, the way that they describe leadership style is broadly the same – people concerns and tasks concerns. Crucially, though, the two styles of behaviour in the Michigan studies were presumed to be at opposite ends of a single dimension. Thus, a leader was thought to exhibit either job-centred or employee-centred leader behaviour, but not both. The Michigan studies added to the picture by finding that the ineffective leader was the one concerned only with the task.

The differences between the Ohio and Michigan studies leave us with some questions. Are effective leaders only concerned with people, or concerned with both task and people? Is concern for both possible?

Much research indicates that this is a complex issue. The early Ohio State studies suggested that considerate leaders were associated with a pleasant group atmosphere and high morale, but were considered less effective by superiors. Because they were reluctant to establish standards or reprimand, output sometimes suffered. Structuring leaders, on the other hand, were associated with lower levels of subordinate job satisfaction but were considered more effective by superiors. Efficiency and performance were sometimes enhanced by this leadership style. So there was a trade off, either high morale or high output with higher superior ratings.

Later researchers argued that leaders who are high on both dimensions can have the best of both worlds. A study by Halpin (1957) of aircraft commanders and school head teachers showed that leaders who scored high on both consideration and structure were seen as more effective by superiors and had high group morale. Blake and Mouton (1964) developed their Managerial Grid, on which an individual can plot his or her own style on the two dimensions of concern for people and concern for production or task and obtain a 'profile'. To be a 'hi-hi' or '9,9' leader, as it became known, is considered the best. Courses have been designed to train and encourage leaders to adopt this style.

In the Leadership Grid, the latest version of the Blake and Mouton Managerial Grid, there are various combinations of concern for people and concern for production which describe five major leadership styles (see Figure 2.1).

1   *Authority/Obedience Management*, or task management, a 9,1 style, emphasizes efficiency in operations that results from arranging work conditions in such a way that human elements can only interfere to a small degree.

2   *Country club management*, or a 1,9 style, involves thoughtful attention to the needs of people, because such satisfying relationships are expected to lead to a comfortable, friendly organizational atmosphere.

3   *Impoverished management*, or *laissez-faire* management, a 1,1 style, is characterized by the exertion of minimum effort to get the required work done and sustain organization membership.

4   *Middle of the road management*, or a 5,5 style, is concerned with balancing the necessity to get the work done while maintaining morale at a satisfactory level. The goal is adequate performance.

5   *Team management*, or a 9,9 style, relies on interdependence through a common stake in the organization's purpose. This interdependence leads to relationships based on mutual trust and respect, and work is accomplished by committed employees.

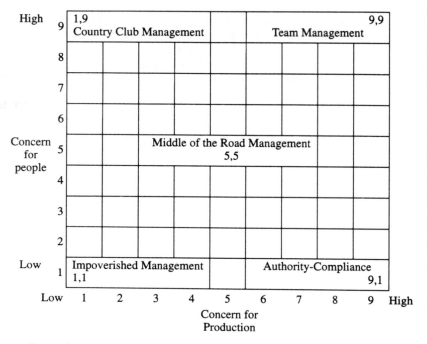

Figure 2.1 The leadership grid
Source: Blake and McCanse (1991).

The Managerial Grid model assumes that there is one best style, the 9,9 one. The most effective leader is supposed to combine concern for people with concern for task. The evidence for this assertion is not convincing. Like other style approaches which specify a set behaviour which is appropriate in all situations, it ignores the fact that such simple panaceas cannot do justice to the enormous complexities of individual behaviour in different organizational settings. Different styles are appropriate in different circumstances. The style adopted by the leader of a fire-fighting team when tackling a blazing building is not likely to be the same as that adopted by a leader of a research and development team testing new anti-asthma drugs. Moreover, the fire-fighter might adopt a different style when training others compared to when he is directing them at a fire, or a different style with a raw recruit compared with an old hand.

PARTICIPATION

Another way of looking at style, and one that was popular in the 1960s and 1970s, is in terms of participation. How participative or how authoritarian is the leader? When looking at leadership behaviour, especially when decision-making, one can think of a continuum along which the behaviours fall. At one extreme the leader tells subordinates, at the other he or she joins with subordinates in making the decision (see Figure 2.2). At one end the leader is task oriented, or authoritarian; he or she uses the authority of the position to make the decision on his or her own. At the other extreme of the continuum, the leader is relationships oriented, or democratic. Here he or she is concerned to allow lots of room for the subordinates to influence the decision which has to be made. Tannenbaum and Schmidt (1958) described the continuum as seven different

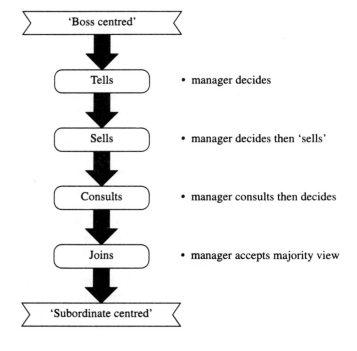

Figure 2.2 The leadership continuum
Source: Tannenbaum and Schmidt (1958).

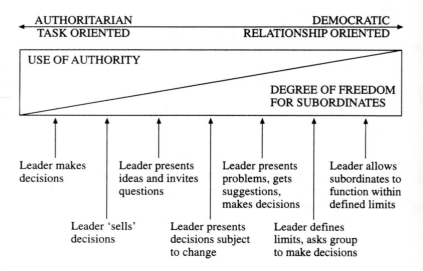

Figure 2.3 Leadership style
Source: Tannenbaum and Schmidt (1958).

behaviours that a leader could choose to adopt, while recognizing that there are shades of participation along the whole scale (see Figure 2.3).

The four degrees of participation model, shown in Figure 2.2, was used by Sadler (1970) to investigate which style employees in a large computer company in Britain perceived and preferred their manager to exhibit, and whether the perceived style was related to sub-ordinates' attitudes. The results are shown in Tables 2.1 and 2.2 and reveal that most of the employees could describe their immediate superior using one of the four style descriptions. Superiors were not seen as falling predominantly into one style or another, although managers saw themselves as more likely to be consulted than were clerical and blue-collar workers. When we look at which style they would *prefer* their boss to use, as opposed to the one they saw their boss as predominantly using, the results are very different from each other. The preferred style is consultative. This is true for all grades of staff, but particularly so for higher grades. Surprisingly, the out and out democratic style is the least preferred by most groups. So employees want to be consulted about decisions, to play a part in

Table 2.1 Leadership styles

	Autocratic (%)		Persuasive (%)		Consult-ative (%)		Democratic (%)		None of these (%)		No reply (%)	
	Perc	Pref	Perc	Pref	Perc	Pref	Perc	Pref	Perc	Pref	Perc	Pref
Managers	15	8	30	16	36	71	6	2	12	–	2	2
Supervisors	34	18	20	31	15	46	8	2	20	–	3	3
Clerical, secretarial	26	14	19	25	18	39	6	16	20	–	10	6
'Blue-collar' workers	23	15	16	19	16	47	5	17	36	–	4	2

Source: Sadler (1970).
Notes: Perc = Perceived leadership style. Pref = Preferred leadership style.

Table 2.2 Attitudes

	Autocratic (%)	Persuasive (%)	Consultative (%)	Democratic (%)	None of these (%)
High job satisfaction	72	81	84	81	66
High satisfaction with organization	86	90	93	87	82
High confidence in management	76	87	89	70	50
High rating of manager's efficiency	38	30	35	27	12

Source: Sadler (1970).

deciding what should happen, but don't look to take over the decision-making completely. They recognize that the leader should have the final say. Satisfaction with the job and the organization is high for all styles, but lowest where the leader has no recognizable style, implying that even autocracy is preferable to a changeable, wishy-washy style. At least you know where you stand with an autocrat, even if you don't like it. Only in ratings of a manager's efficiency does the autocratic style just creep ahead.

The style approach generally, and the participative research exemplified by Sadler and Barry, viewed styles as points on a continuum or dimension. More recently Muczyk and Reimann (1987) argued that there are really two dimensions. One concerns the extent to which leaders allow subordinates to get involved in decision-making. This is the *autocratic–democratic* dimension. The other is concerned with the extent to which leaders tell subordinates how to do their jobs and direct their activities. This is the *permissive–directive* dimension. If these two are considered separate and independent of each other, then we can describe leaders as predominantly one of four types. These are:

1   directive autocrat;
2   permissive autocrat;
3   directive democrat;
4   permissive democrat.

The obvious next question is whether one type or style is superior to another. As you may have guessed by now, it all depends. Directive autocrats may sound most unpleasant people to work for. They make decisions unilaterally and closely supervise the work of those who report to them. But they can be respected and effective in certain situations, such as when a subordinate is new to the job and uncertain of what to do or how to do it. Once the subordinate has learned the work and feels more confident, then the style becomes inappropriate. At the other extreme is the permissive democrat. Here the leader makes decisions participatively and allows subordinates considerable freedom to carry out assigned tasks as they see fit. To confident, skilled and knowledgeable individuals who want to perform as best they can, this style may be just what they are seeking. But in other circumstances it can be ineffective and very unsettling for the subordinate, as I know from personal experience. A few years ago I supervised the Ph.D. research of a student from the developing world. My style when supervising doctoral students might be described as permissive democrat. It works well enough with most students, but in this case I soon learned it was drastically wrong. The culture and training of my new student led him to expect a much more autocratic style, where I would closely supervise him throughout the three-year period. Nor did he particularly want to be involved in decision-making. He wanted and expected a directive autocrat. In the end we compromised by me adopting a directive democratic style. I insisted that we made decisions participatively. After all, it was his research he was developing. But he got me to supervise much more closely than I would normally believe to be in the student's best interests. Changing one's preferred style is not easy for either party.

CRITICISMS OF THE STYLE APPROACH

There have been a number of criticisms of the style approach, among them (1) the problem of causality, (2) the problem of the group, (3) informal leadership, and (4) the absence of situational analysis. Bryman (1992) gives a useful review of these criticisms.

The problem of causality

This applies just as much to the trait approach as to the style approach. The assumption in much of the literature is that leader style *causes* various outcomes such as productivity, satisfaction or morale. Yet most research in this area is cross sectional; data on both leader style, and the dependent variable such as output, are collected at the same time and then correlated. Just because two variables are correlated does not mean that one causes the other. So we cannot claim that leadership style causes high output. It is just as likely that high output causes a certain leadership style, since one can easily imagine leaders adjusting their style in response to the group output or the job satisfaction of subordinates. Or both style and output could be caused by a third variable, say advanced technology.

It is only by using longitudinal studies that the causal direction can be examined. A study by Greene (1975) is one of just a handful of such investigations. Greene collected data at three one-month intervals so as to be able to measure any effects of leader behaviour over time. Results showed that highly considerate leaders led to greater subordinate satisfaction, much as we would have expected. But output, that is the quality and quantity of subordinates' work, affected the behaviour of the leader. Poor subordinate performance led the leader to use a predominantly structuring style. So it looks as if performance problems lead to structuring behaviour, rather than the other way round. Greene's study suggests that output influences leadership style rather than supporting the more common assumption that the leadership style influences the output.

The problem of the group

The problem of the group lies in the fact that much of the concern of leadership theory lies in the relationship between the leader and the group, while much of the data collected in the style approach is an averaging of the responses of individual group members. The process whereby subordinates complete questionnaires describing their immediate superior and the researcher then averages the responses, ignores or conceals the fact that a leader may behave very differently towards one individual compared to another. Some research has shown that individual responses to a leader predict feelings of satisfaction and the clarity with which subordinates understand their roles much better than simply averaging the group's responses (Katerberg and Hom, 1981). Much of the behaviour approach to leadership ignores differences between subordinates in their descriptions of their leader.

Informal leadership

Much of the research on leadership behaviour ignores the issue of informal leadership. The reality of organizational life is that employees often recognize someone as their leader, or are influenced by someone, who is not the formal leader as given in an organization chart. Such a person is known as the informal leader. The term also includes groups of peers, such as temporary student project groups, or an informal gathering of friends, where there is no designated leader but where people can easily agree on who tends to take the lead. Most of the studies examining leadership style focus on the designated leader of the group – that is, the one in the formal leadership position. So they may be focusing on the wrong person. Leadership is about influence, as we saw in Chapter 1, and the formal leader may not be the one with the influence in the minds of the subordinates. If the styles of the formal and informal leader differ, erroneous conclusions on the impact of leadership style can result.

The absence of situational analysis

This concerns the failure of the style approach to pay sufficient attention to variables which may moderate the relationship between behaviour and outcome, such as satisfaction and performance. Potentially there are numerous such mediating variables. They include subordinates' experience, motivation and knowledge; the size, business sector and technology of the organization; the nature of the work; the organizational culture; and environmental factors such as the economic cycle and the country in which the organization is situated.

There have been attempts to bring situational variables into the original Ohio State findings. Schriesheim and Murphy (1976) used a recent version of the Ohio State questionnaire in a study of a social services organization. They showed that when jobs are stressful, greater initiation of structure improves subordinate performance but reduces performance when jobs are not stressful.

SUMMARY

Recent research suggests that successful leaders may possess certain traits which distinguish them from followers, although only a small number of traits may be involved. Yet no clear distinction has been established between *effective* and *ineffective* leaders in relation to traits. Concerning styles of leadership, research shows that while one style may be better than another in some cases, no one single style of leadership is appropriate in all circumstances. There are also criticisms of the style approach. The failure to consider situational factors adequately is the most serious problem with the style approach to leadership. It was attempts to address the situational issue which ushered in the next major phase in the progress of leadership research – the contingency approach.

3 Contingency approaches

Contingency approaches have in common that they attempt to address the question: When is one type of leadership behaviour more appropriate than another? The answer is, it all depends. Style or behaviour is dependent (contingent) upon the context. What variables are considered as 'the context' varies from one contingency model to another. Although many of the behavioural approaches to leadership saw that there was no one best style for all situations, it is the contingency models which attempt to establish *how* the situation changes the behaviour. So contingency theories are complex. They have to set out which leader behaviours should change, which aspects of the context are most crucial, and how the specific leader behaviour and the situation interact.

In this chapter we will look at some of the more influential contingency theories, namely the Situational Leadership Theory of Hersey and Blanchard; Fiedler's Contingency Theory; the Vroom–Yetton–Jago Normative Model, and House's Path–Goal Theory.

SITUATIONAL LEADERSHIP THEORY

Quite often in occupational psychology we find that theories which capture the imagination of practising managers and management trainers are not the ones which, on investigation, are strongly supported by empirical evidence. Hersey and Blanchard's Situational Leadership Theory is one such example. It is widely used on management development courses, presumably because it strikes a cord with the audience, is prescriptive and has intuitive appeal. It *seems* to be giving form to what managers have learned through experience, and offers them a language to analyse those experiences.

As we will see later, though, the evidence supporting the theory is not strong.

It is also appropriate that we start the chapter on contingency theories with one which bases its key concepts on the main findings of the style approaches of the Ohio State and Michigan studies. Situational Leadership Theory takes as its starting point the fact that there are two dimensions of leader behaviour: relationship behaviours and task behaviours. These are independent of each other. Relationship behaviour is the amount of support, recognition and personal encouragement the leader extends to subordinates. Task behaviour is the amount of direction and structure the leader provides. Since the two dimensions are independent of each other, we can think of four typical leadership styles in a 2×2 matrix, as shown in Figure 3.1. These four styles are structuring, coaching, encouraging and delegating. The assumption is that there is no one best style. On the contrary, one type of behaviour is more appropriate in one situation than another. By using relationship and task behaviour in differing amounts at different times a leader can help subordinates become more productive and fulfilled in their jobs.

By 'situation' in Situational Leadership Theory, Hersey and Blanchard mean:

- the willingness of people to do their work assignments;
- the ability of people to do their work assignments;
- the nature of the work they do;
- the climate of the organization.

Although some reference is made in the theory to the last two categories in this list, it is the characteristics of subordinates, not the work itself or the external and internal environment of the organization, which the theory mostly concentrates on. A key variable here is follower maturity (called 'readiness' in some versions of the theory). Follower maturity refers to the subordinates' understanding of the job and commitment to it (see Table 3.1). When a subordinate has low levels of maturity, high task and low relationship behaviour is seen as being the best combination. This is the structuring style. As subordinate maturity grows, the need for relationship-type behaviour on the part of the leader increases and task behaviour declines. At the highest level of maturity, high levels of relationship or task behaviour are unnecessary for employee performance, and may get in the way.

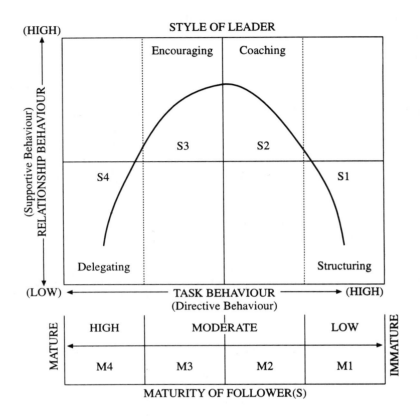

Figure 3.1 Situational leadership
Source: Hersey and Blanchard (1988).

This is the delegating style. Maturity applies to a task, not to a person. Someone may have high maturity for one task and low maturity for another. Take the job of a secretary as an example. She may need no guidance on word processing, writing a standard memo, or laying out a document, so a delegating style would be most appropriate. But say she is asked, for the first time, to use the computerized information retrieval system in the library, to look up books and articles. For this task, a structuring style with clear guidance, advice and demonstration may be appropriate until such times as she feels confident enough to do it with minimal telling and encouragement. It is for this

Table 3.1 Maturity

1 Job maturity dimensions	1.1	Previous experience
	1.2	Current knowledge
	1.3	Meeting deadlines
	1.4	Ability to take responsibility
	1.5	Problem-solving ability
	1.6	Awareness of political implications
2 Psychological maturity dimensions	2.1	Persistence
	2.2	Independence
	2.3	Achievement orientation
	2.4	Attitude to work
	2.5	Willingness to take responsibility

Source: Hersey and Blanchard (1988).
Note: Maturity = job maturity + psychological maturity defined for a particular task.

reason that Figure 3.1 shows a bell-shaped curve. The model argues that for a particular task, an employee may start in the S1 box and move through S2 and S3 to S4, over time. For many tasks, a subordinate may never reach S4, due perhaps to lack of opportunity to learn the task and feel sufficiently confident to tackle it when it is delegated.

Evidence

As noted at the start of this section, Situational Leadership Theory has considerable intuitive appeal. Unfortunately, the empirical evidence is thin in support of its assumptions about changing leadership style with increased subordinate maturity. It is not so much that empirical evidence fails to support it. It is more the fact that the theory has not generated much research.

A study by Vecchio (1987) provides limited support. Vecchio asked 303 high school teachers in the USA to complete questionnaires giving their perceptions of head teachers' behaviour. The questionnaire was principally concerned with relationships and task orientation. They also reported on the quality of their relationship with the head teacher and their satisfaction with the head's leadership. The head teachers themselves rated the maturity and job performance of their staff.

Situational Leadership Theory predicts that subordinates will perform best, and have the highest levels of satisfaction, when their leader's style matches their level of maturity. The results showed that this prediction was only partially supported. Subordinates whose leader's style matched their maturity level were indeed more satisfied and received higher performance ratings than those subordinates where there was no match. But the results depended on the teachers' level of maturity. The theory's predictions were most accurate for subordinates with low maturity, reasonably accurate for those with moderate maturity and not at all accurate for those with high maturity.

These results suggest that Situational Leadership Theory may be most applicable for those subordinates with low levels of maturity. For new employees, or those with low task-relevant knowledge and experience, a structuring approach might well be best. It is associated with higher levels of satisfaction and better performance on the part of employees. But the crucial finding is that where subordinates are mature, it is still appropriate to use relationships and task behaviour as least some of the time. Without it, satisfaction and performance might well fall off.

FIEDLER'S CONTINGENCY THEORY

Fiedler developed one of the first true contingency theories of the leadership process (Fiedler, 1967). The theory states that leader performance is contingent upon both the leader's personal characteristics and the degree to which the leader controls the situation. The personal characteristics comprise a motivational system, according to Fiedler, and concern how positively the leader views his or her *least preferred co-worker* (LPC). The LPC is a key variable in the theory. Leaders are asked to nominate the person they have least liked, of all those they have worked with. This becomes the least preferred co-worker. This person is then rated on a set of eighteen 8-point scales, such as:

$$\text{Friendly} - - - - - - - - \text{Unfriendly}$$
$$\phantom{\text{Friendly}} 8 \quad 7 \quad 6 \quad 5 \quad 4 \quad 3 \quad 2 \quad 1$$

$$\text{Considerate} - - - - - - - - \text{Inconsiderate}$$
$$\phantom{\text{Considerate}} 8 \quad 7 \quad 6 \quad 5 \quad 4 \quad 3 \quad 2 \quad 1$$

A low LPC score means that leaders describe their least preferred co-worker in negative terms, while a high LPC score indicates a more positive description. High LPC leaders are classified as relationships, or people, oriented (they tend to feel fairly positive even about people they don't like very much); low LPC individuals are classified as task oriented.

In addition to the LPC, there are three contingency variables. These are group atmosphere, task structure and the leader's position power. They determine the degree to which the situation is favourable to the leader by providing *control* over subordinates.

Group atmosphere refers to the extent to which the leader enjoys the support and loyalty of group members. It describes how accepted the leader is by the team. In groups that reject the leader, the task is unlikely to get done, since the group will attempt to sabotage or ignore the task as given. In groups which support the leader, members are likely to commit themselves to the task. There is no need for the leader to pull rank or jump up and down to attempt to get the job done.

Task structure refers to the degree to which the task, its goals and the roles of subordinates are clearly defined. A routine task, such as filing, is likely to have clearly defined goals (file all correspondence alphabetically by client's surname and then chronologically in date order), consist of a few steps (retrieve from unsorted pile, open filing cabinet, place in correct file) and have a correct solution (Smith goes before Smithers who goes before Smurfitt). Completely non-routine tasks are at the other extreme. The leader may know no more than the rest of the group how to solve the problem. Such a task is likely to have unclear goals, multiple paths to accomplishment and uncertain success criteria. Raising the attractiveness of an organization's image so as to attract better applicants might be one example. How do we know when we have succeeded? How do we do it? How do we know that we caused the change rather than other factors, such as increased attractiveness by paying more or more people unemployed and looking for work? These are just some of the questions to which there may be no clear-cut, satisfactory answer. Routine versus non-routine tasks will require very different leader behaviours.

Position power is the power inherent in the leader's role. It is the extent to which a leader controls rewards and punishments for subordinates. In many industrial and commercial organizations in Britain, leaders have fairly high position power. They can recruit,

	1	2	3	4	5	6	7	8
Group atmosphere	Good	Good	Good	Good	Poor	Poor	Poor	Poor
Task structure	High	High	Low	Low	High	High	Low	Low
Leader position power	Strong	Weak	Strong	Weak	Strong	Weak	Strong	Weak
Desirable leader	Low LPC	Low LPC	Low LPC	High LPC	High LPC	High LPC	High LPC	Low LPC

Most favourable situation for leader _____ Least favourable situation for leader

Figure 3.2 Fiedler's Contingency Theory

dismiss, promote and financially reward employees, assuming they follow the rules, procedures or guidelines laid down by the law and regulatory bodies. In public sector organizations, such as universities and the civil service, leaders typically have lower position power. They are more constrained by the organization culture, which encourages consultation, and by laws and agreements set out by governments or unions.

Fiedler divides the three variables into high and low, and combines them as shown in Figure 3.2. This basic contingency model shows the results from Fiedler's early research. The research indicates that where the situation was either favourable to the leader (situations 1, 2 and 3) or highly unfavourable (situation 8), group performance was best if the leader had a low LPC score (i.e. was task oriented). In contrast, situations which were moderate or low in favourability to the leader, high LPC scores (i.e. person oriented leaders) had the best group performance. Favourable or unfavourable situations refer to the extent to which the leader has control over the situation.

What is not known for sure is *why* high LPC leaders should be more effective in moderately favourable situations, while low LPC leaders are more effective in the remaining extreme situations. The most popular explanation is still the original one put forward by Fiedler when he first described the model. When the situation is good, the leader does not *need* to spend time on relationships with others. So task oriented leaders, who prefer to spend time and effort on the task, are more effective. All the situation requires is persistence and a concentration on the task. In extremely difficult situations, things are so bad that it is not *worth* spending time on relationships with others. What is needed is a firm, task oriented leader. If anything is going to be achieved in such unfavourable circumstances then the leader must concentrate wholeheartedly on results. In situations that are not at the extremes of favourability or unfavourability, leaders can and should apply interpersonal skills to keep people happy and to overcome obstacles. High people orientation is required here.

An alternative explanation is that the findings reflect a matching of the leader with the situation. It is argued that high LPC individuals are cognitively complex. That is, they are able to perceive the world and the people in it in many different ways and in shades of grey, rather than simplistically and as black and white. Low LPC individuals, on the other hand, are more cognitively simple. They judge people and events in simplistic terms, as good or bad, like or dislike, right or wrong. They miss the complexities, subtleties and shades of difference in people and events. Cognitive complexity reveals itself in the LPC questionnaire. Those individuals who give some positive ratings, as well as some negative ratings, to their least preferred co-worker end up classified as high LPC leaders. Those for whom the least preferred co-worker is all bad are the low LPC leaders.

Situations too, so the argument goes, can be seen as relatively simple or relatively complex. Simple situations are those where all the features are reasonably congruent – that is, all good or all bad. Simple situations are at the ends of the spectrum in the contingency model in Figure 3.2. Complex situations are those where the features are mixed, as in the middle section of the figure.

The 'matching' explanation for the Fiedler results states that the findings reflect the matching of leader cognitive complexity with situational complexity. Cognitively complex individuals make better leaders in relatively complex situations. Individuals who are more cognitively simple do better in simple situations.

A basic premise of the theory is that leadership behaviour is a personality trait and so an individual's LPC score is relatively stable. Because of this, there is very little point in trying to change a leader's style by training or development opportunities. It is more sensible to match a leader's style with the situation, rather than expect the individual to change to adapt to different situations. When a leader's style and the situation do not match, the only available course of action is to change the situation or change the leader. There is even a computer program which can be used to match leader and situation. Fiedler suggests that a leader should deliberately try to change the situation favourableness by enhancing relations with subordinates, changing the amount of structure in a task, or gaining more formal power. The aim is to improve group performance by making the situation more closely fit one's personal leadership style.

The evidence

As with any theory, the key question is, how well does it fare when compared with the empirical evidence? The answer is reasonably well. A meta-analysis of 170 studies that had tested the theory up to 1981 (Strube and Garcia, 1981), and a similar study in 1985 (Peters *et al.*, 1985) showed that most of them had obtained positive results. Peters *et al.* concluded that the data on which the theory was originally based supported the theory very well. Later studies have provided more support, though sometimes less conclusively.

One example of a supporting study is by Chemers *et al.* (1985). They tested the proposition that leaders whose style did not match the situation would experience greater job-related stress than leaders whose style did match the conditions. For example, they predicted that high LPC (relationships oriented) leaders with high or low situational control (high or low favourability) would show higher stress levels than low LPC (task oriented) leaders in these conditions. Similarly, low LPC individuals with moderate situational control would show higher stress than high LPC individuals in those conditions.

Chemers and his colleagues asked university administrators to complete questionnaires designed to measure their LPC score, the degree of situational control and the level of job stress they felt. The results supported the predictions. Those administrators whose personal style did not match the level of situational control reported greater levels of job stress than those where style matched the situation.

The evidence on the theory suggests that laboratory based studies have produced results more supportive of the theory than have field based studies.

Problems with Fiedler's contingency theory

A number of problems have been pointed out with regard to Fiedler's theory (e.g. Ashour, 1973; Peters *et al.*, 1985).

1   Some have criticized the LPC concept, arguing that it is one-dimensional and that better measures of leadership behaviour are required. The one-dimensional nature of the LPC implies that if leaders are highly motivated to accomplish the task they are not concerned with relations among employees, and vice versa. But as we have seen from the Ohio State studies and others, leaders can be high or low on both.

2   The reliability of the LPC questionnaire does not seem to be as high as is normally demanded of such instruments. So there is doubt about whether the LPC scores are as stable as Fiedler maintains. Much may depend on just how awful the least preferred co-worker really is!

3   It is not always clear how specific situations can be classified along the dimension of situational control. Unless situations can be classified unambiguously as very high, high, moderate, and so on, it is difficult to make predictions about which style will be most effective.

4   The model does not consider that leaders can influence both the task structure and the group atmosphere from their knowledge of the situation. So the task can be changed by the leader and should not be seen as a dependent variable in the model. The nature of the employee's task can be determined in part by the style of the leader.

5   There is a lack of evidence for *why* the model is as it is. The model is a 'black box'. Until it is better supported by good explanations, the model must be viewed with some caution.

THE VROOM–YETTON–JAGO NORMATIVE MODEL

Much of what leaders do involves making decisions. That is true, of course, for everyone, not only leaders. As I write this chapter, I am making decisions all the time: about what to include and what to leave out, how to phrase what I write, and so on. When you got up this morning, you made decisions about when to do so, what to have for breakfast, or whether to skip breakfast altogether, and hundreds of other decisions you are hardly aware of. But what characterizes

Table 3.2   Leadership decision styles

Here are five styles which you, acting as a leader, might use in reaching a decision. They differ only in the amount of participation which you allow your subordinates and thus the degree to which they can influence the final decision. 'Subordinates' refers to those who report *directly* to you.

Note that with each style, you take full responsibility. *In no case* do you give up either the authority or responsibility for the final decision.

Style	Description
AI	*You decide alone.* You make the decision without discussing the situation with anyone. You rely entirely on personal knowledge or information available in written documents.
AII	*You seek information and then decide alone.* You seek additional information from one or more of your subordinates to arrive at a decision. You may or may not describe the problem to them, but you solicit information only, not solutions or suggestions.
CI	*You consult with individuals and then decide alone.* Here you share the problem with selected subordinates, individually. You gather additional information from them and seek their advice about possible solutions to the problem. Still, you make the decision.
CII	*You consult with your entire group and then decide alone.* Using this style, you meet with your subordinates in a group and discuss the possible alternatives, essentially using them as consultants. You may use their feelings and opinions as additional input, but you retain the final decision power.
GII	*You share the problem with your group, and you all mutually decide what to do.* Here you give your subordinates full participation in the decision-making process. You may define the problem for them, provide relevant information, and participate in the discussion as any other member, but you do not use your position as leader to influence them. The group is the decision-maker, and you accept not only its decision, but also the responsibility for it. Your description to others will be 'We decided to …', not 'The group decided to …', or 'I decided to …'

Source: Adapted from Vroom and Yetton (1973).

leadership decision-making is the involvement of followers, and the fact that usually the final responsibility rests with the leader. The motto on the desk of Harry S. Truman reading 'the buck stops here' doesn't only apply to US presidents.

Vroom and Yetton (1973) developed a contingency theory of leadership decision-making. This addressed the question of how much leaders should involve subordinates in decision-making. It is a normative theory because it sets out rules that it proposes leaders should follow in order to make the best decisions in the circumstances. The original theory was updated and extended by Vroom and Jago (1988).

Vroom and Yetton proposed that leaders usually adopt one of five distinct methods for reaching decisions. These are set out in Table 3.2. The five methods reflect a continuum ranging from highly autocratic to highly participative approaches. The AI category refers to Autocratic I, where the leader chooses to make the decision alone. The roman numeral I or II refers to the degree of autocracy. AII is similar, but the leader requests information from others before deciding alone. CI refers to Consultation 1, and involves sharing the problem with others on a one-to-one basis. Again, CII is similar, but the leader consults others in a group setting. G is short for Group and GII refers to group decision-making with consensus as the goal.

Vroom and Yetton gave seven key questions that leaders should consider when making a decision:

1   QR (*Quality Requirement*)
    Is there a quality consideration which indicates one solution produces a better outcome?
2   CR (*Commitment Requirement*)
    Is the commitment of followers critical to effective implementation?
3   LI (*Leader Information*)
    Does the leader have the information needed to make a good decision?
4   PS (*Problem Structure*)
    Is the problem well structured, e.g. does the leader know which followers to contact?
5   CP (*Commitment Probability*)
    If the leader decides alone, is it reasonably certain that the decision would be accepted by followers?

6   *GC* (*Goal Congruence*)
Do followers share the organizational goals to be obtained in solving this problem?

7   *CO* (*Subordinate Conflict*)
Is conflict among followers over preferred solutions likely?

The theory addresses the issue of how a leader should choose one decision style rather than another. It does not suggest one best style. Rather, it points to questions leaders should ask themselves before involving others. Answering those questions is a balancing act between a number of variables, especially time, decision quality and subordinate satisfaction and development. The more autocratic end of the spectrum means that the leader makes the decision quickly. No one is involved but the leader. In certain circumstances this is the best approach. In emergencies, for example, the best decision may be the quickest. Where the leader has all the information required and the subordinates are not bothered about the outcome, it is a waste of time to involve them. On the other hand, there will be many times when others should be involved in decision-making, especially when their contribution is valuable, say when they have technical information to offer. At other times, too, subordinates may expect or want to be involved in matters which affect them or over which they feel they have a right to make an input. A decision to change the core hours that employees should be in the office under a flexitime system is an example. It might be quickest in the short term for the departmental manager alone to make the decision (AI) or get information from subordinates on what times they could be in and need to leave to catch buses and trains, and then decide (AII). However, to get an optimum decision that suits everyone best would necessitate consulting the team. Then come other decisions. Meet in a group (CII) or singly one-to-one (CI)? Is the manager prepared to accept the group consensus (GII), even if it doesn't suit him or her or won't be easily accepted by superiors?

In order to work a way through this decision-making conundrum, Vroom and Yetton set out seven rules. These help leaders eliminate decision-making strategies that are likely to prove ineffective in a given situation and select those likely to be more effective. Three rules are concerned with the quality of the decision and four have to do with the decision acceptance by subordinates. Bob Dorn of the Center for Creative Leadership in Greensboro, North Carolina, USA, explains quality and commitment issues as follows.

Quality

Quality refers to the 'correctness' of the decision itself, regardless of the reaction of the subordinates to it. If one solution to a problem is equally effective or efficient and would cost less, or if one method or product would meet the client's needs or sell better than another at the same cost, then that would be the highest quality solution. Quality depends entirely on the decision-maker(s) having sufficient and accurate information on which to base the decision.

Opinions or factual information on how well subordinates would like one solution rather than another would not be relevant information which should influence the quality of the decision. That information is relevant to *acceptance* but not to the *quality* of the decision. The model deals with the two issues separately.

Compliance versus commitment

The model assumes that subordinates will comply with – that is, not openly refuse to implement – any decision of the leader. *Compliance* therefore is guaranteed. But it could result in faulty implementation. This can range from no implementation without direct supervision or closely monitored performance, to grudging implementation at minimum standards of performance.

Compliance is sufficient only when appropriate implementation of the decision would involve no initiative or creativity, and for which performance could always be closely monitored. For tasks such as using a different version of a simple reporting form, punching in and out at a different time on the time-clock, and performing a routine task at a different location, compliance would be sufficient.

Complete acceptance, on the other hand, produces wholehearted *commitment*. This results in enthusiastic, creative, self-directed, vigorous implementation to the best of the follower's ability. Among the variables likely to bring about commitment as opposed to compliance are those when the leader is viewed as both an expert and as one who cares about the welfare of subordinates and when the followers have a hand in making the decision.

The model provides a guide to help the leader produce a high-quality decision in the shortest possible time using the method that will promote the degree of acceptance needed for appropriate implementation. It assumes that:

- Quality reaches its peak when all available relevant information and opinions have been examined.
- Time to produce a decision increases as one goes from AI to GII.
- Acceptance, if uncertain, increases as one moves from AI to GII.
- GII is not a viable option if the leader and the group are likely to have conflicting views or desires relative to the quality issue.

In the original Vroom and Yetton model, there were seven rules (see pp. 33–4). A Yes/No answer was required for each question. According to the answer given, a path could be traced through a decision tree which allowed the leader to exclude certain decision-making options and gave the optimum leader style or styles. In many cases more than one style is appropriate. This is set out in Figure 3.3.

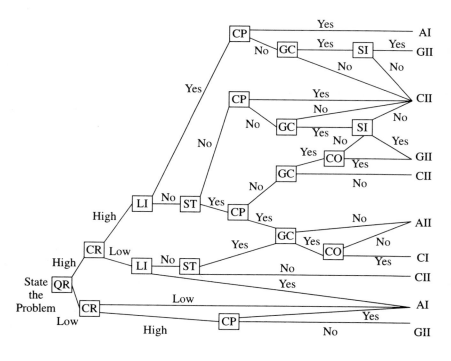

Figure 3.3 The Vroom–Yetton–Jago model
Source: Vroom and Jago (1988).

The revision of the model undertaken by Vroom and Jago (1988) added three more questions, namely:

- Subordinate information: do subordinates have enough information to make a good decision?
- Time constraint: is time too short to involve subordinates in decision-making?
- Geographical dispersion: would it be too expensive to bring together geographically dispersed subordinates?

They also introduced 5-point scales for most questions rather than a simple Yes/No answer, and mathematical formulae so that the optimum style can be found. There is now a computer program available to do the calculations so that leaders can simply input their answers and be given a customized 'suitability score' for each decision style.

The evidence

The Vroom–Yetton model offers clear guidance for choosing one leadership style over another when making decisions. The question is, though, is it valid? Are leaders who choose the approach recommended by the model more effective than those who don't? The evidence is not too clear cut but much of it does support the model.

Vroom and Jago (1978) provided evidence that managers rate their own past decision as more successful when they adopted one of the approaches recommended by the model than they did when they practised one of the approaches which fell outside of the feasible set recommended by the model. 'Feasible set' means one of the prescribed cluster of decision styles specified by the model for that type of problem. In the original Vroom–Yetton model, a particular problem might indicate feasible set 6, suggesting the need for CI or CII behaviours. Feasible set 2 in the revised Vroom–Jago model suggests GII (see Figure 3.3). Ninety-six managers were asked to describe one successful and one unsuccessful decision-making situation they had been involved in. In 65 per cent of the cases the decision-making process they adopted conformed to one of the feasible methods given by the model. Of this 65 per cent, more than two-thirds were successful decisions. By contrast, less than a quarter of the decisions were successful for those managers whose accounts of their behaviour were not within the feasible set given by the model. So the evidence from this study indicates that decision-makers whose behaviour coincided with one of the possible options of the model were more likely to report their decision process as successful.

A rather different study in the UK cleaning industry came to similar conclusions. Margerison and Glube (1979) used case studies that managers were asked to respond to. Managers whose chosen style on the cases tended to agree with the recommendations of the model had firms with higher productivity and workers who were more satisfied with the supervision. This is the case even when the leaders have had no formal training in the model.

Finally, there have been some experimental studies. Field (1982) used business students as subjects. They were divided into small groups comprising a leader, two subordinates and an observer. They were asked to solve case-study problems using one of the five methods described in the model (see Table 3.2). In addition, when the 'leader' made decisions by methods falling inside the feasible set, those decisions were seen as more effective by the observers than when those decisions were reached by other methods.

Problems with the Vroom–Yetton–Jago theory

Much of the evidence supports the Vroom–Yetton model well. Since the Vroom–Jago revised version has not been in existence very long, it is too early to say whether the same support will be forthcoming for this version. But since the two versions are not too dissimilar, it seems likely that there will soon be empirical support for the model. To the extent that the revised model takes on board some of the criticisms and limitations of the earlier version, it may even be more strongly supported. However, the model does have problems.

1   Much of the research hinges on leaders' *recall* and *self reports*. The same individuals are asked which decision-making method they chose and the quality and acceptability of the decision. So there is scope for bias. The success or failure of the decision that leaders have made may well affect their judgement about the methods used to make it and their recall about the nature of the situation and the events which preceded the decision. If I recognize that the decision I made was a good one, and my subordinates were satisfied with the result, I may selectively remember, or kid myself, that I chose this method (perhaps

conforming to the model) rather than any other. This may inflate the validity of the model, a point Vroom himself has acknowledged (Vroom, 1984).

2   Another awkward finding is that *subordinates prefer a participative approach* even when the model suggests a more autocratic approach. Leaders tend to prefer those methods recommended by the normative model whereas subordinates tend to prefer more participative methods whatever the model suggests in those circumstances (Heilman *et al.*, 1984). This may be because subordinates want to influence decisions which affect their jobs, whatever the nature of those decisions.

3   Closely allied to this point, but a different one, is that the model may be *more applicable to managers than to subordinates*. Work by Field and House (1990) asked both managers and subordinates for their reactions to some recent decisions. Both subordinates and managers agreed on the Vroom–Yetton decision method adopted and the effectiveness of the decision. When the manager used one of the feasible set they thought the decisions were more effective than when they did not adopt one of the feasible set. But subordinates did not agree. They did not rate managers' decisions any more effective, whether the strategy was from the feasible set or not. The investigators point to the differing role of managers and subordinates. Subordinates dislike managers' autocratic style even when this is indicated by the model as the most effective.

4   It has been suggested that a *leader's skill* in putting the chosen decision-making method into action may be just as important as the choice of decision style in the first place (Tjosvold *et al.*, 1986). An inappropriate decision method, exercised with skill, may be just as effective as an appropriate decision style exercised only reasonably well. It may be that with the normative model it's not what you do but the way that you do it. Similarly, it has been found that only managers with strongly developed skills in conflict handling are effective with participative methods of decision-making recommended by the model. Managers with low skill are more effective with autocratic styles, though these are not suggested by the model.

In conclusion, there is much research which supports the model, and in this respect it is better supported than many of the leadership theories we have looked at so far. Certainly it seems to be reasonably well supported by managers' accounts of how they make successful decisions, even if subordinates consistently prefer more participation. It is a complex model, made more so by the recent modifications. The new model is, though, more sensitive to differences in the situation and more specific than the original. The advent of computer software to help managers decide on appropriate behaviour when making decisions is an intriguing training tool. Yet just understanding the variables may be enough. It is often used as such in leadership training and development. The model does throw light on our understanding of leader decision-making and can be helpful to both theoreticians and practising managers.

PATH–GOAL THEORY

Another contingency approach is path–goal theory, developed by House and others. It takes expectancy theory as its starting point, which House then adapted to leadership theory.

Expectancy theory concerns itself with the process of motivation. It states that people choose what to do in a given circumstance based on a calculation of the expectancy, instrumentality and valence in the situation.

- *Expectancy* is the belief that your effort will result in performance.
- *Instrumentality* is the belief that your performance will be rewarded.
- *Valence* is how much you value the reward or outcome.

Let's take an example. Expectancy theory says that the motivation or effort you expend to pass an exam depends on the extent to which you:

- Believe that even if you tried hard, worked lots of hours and concentrated fully, you would not get a good mark (expectancy). You may feel that even with work, you are not bright enough to pass.
- Believe that through putting in the effort you would get a fair mark, so that your effort will result (be instrumental) in you getting a better mark than you would have got. You may feel that exam nerves or poor exam technique has always resulted in you getting poor marks, so why bother too much.
- The value (valence) you place on getting a good mark. You have to

value studying for this exam over doing other things, such as drinking coffee, chatting or going out.

Your effort or motivation, your force to act, can be calculated by multiplying the three factors. So if any one of them is zero (you don't value exam passes, say), then your motivation is zero.

The fundamental tenet of path–goal theory is that subordinates will react favourably to a leader to the extent that they perceive and calculate that she or he will help them to attain goals. If a leader clarifies the nature of the tasks and smooths the path to the goal by reducing or eliminating obstacles, then the subordinates will work hard. This is because they perceive (have an expectancy) that working hard leads to (is instrumental in) high performance, and high performance leads to valued rewards (the rewards have high valence) such as pay or status.

The theory states that there are four types of leader behaviour which can affect motivation of subordinates:

1   *Instrumental leadership* (sometimes called 'directive'). This involves giving specific guidance to subordinates, clarifying their role, asking them to follow standard rules, explaining how work should be accomplished, and so on. It is similar to the high-structure, low-consideration style in the Ohio studies or the high-task, low-people approach in the Situational Leadership model of Hersey and Blanchard or the Managerial Grid of Blake and Mouton.

2   *Supportive leadership.* This involves being friendly and approachable to subordinates, sensitive to their needs, and concerned for their well-being and status. It is similar to the low-structure, high-consideration of the Ohio studies or the low-task, high-people approach of the Managerial Grid or the Situational Leadership model.

2   *Participative leadership.* This involves sharing information with subordinates, consulting with them and involving them before making decisions. It is like the high/high of the Ohio studies, the Managerial Grid or the Situational Leadership model.

3   *Achievement-oriented leadership.* This involves setting challenging goals and emphasizing excellence while simultaneously showing confidence in subordinates' ability to achieve those high goals.

House points out that all of these four styles can be used by a single leader, depending on the circumstances. Showing such flexibility is, in fact, one feature of an effective leader.

Which category is best for subordinate satisfaction and perform-ance is dependent on two broad contingency factors. The first of these is the *characteristics of subordinates*. A subordinate's attributes affect whether he or she sees the leader's behaviour as leading to the satisfaction of his or her goals, either now or in the future. Some of the personal characteristics proposed by the theory are locus of control, perceived ability and affiliation needs.

Locus of control refers to whether someone believes that what happens to them is the result of their own behaviour or is the result of forces outside of their own control. There is research evidence that internals are more satisfied with a participative leader, while externals are more satisfied with a directive leader (Mitchell, 1973). If I believe that what happens to me is my own responsibility, then I am more likely to respond well to someone who gives me a chance to shape what it is that I do. I am likely to believe that I have the best chance of attaining my own goals if it is left to me rather than have someone else directing me. If, on the other hand, I believe that fate and power play a large part in determining what happens to me, I am likely to feel quite comfortable letting others take control. I will believe that this is the best way to achieve my goals.

Perceived ability refers to how people see their own ability relative to a specific task. Subordinates who rate their ability highly are less likely to accept directive leadership. This is explained by the simple reasoning that if I feel that I am good at something, why would I want someone else to tell me how to do it? 'I know how to do it, so leave me to get on with it!' If, on the other hand, I am uncertain of, or unconfident in, my skills, I will probably appreciate all the help and direction I can get in order to attain my goals.

Similarly, those who have strong needs for achievement may prefer leaders who are achievement oriented. Those who have strong *needs for affiliation* (like close, friendly ties with others) are likely to prefer participative and supportive leaders.

The second broad contingency factor considered by the path–goal theory is the *work environment*. This includes the task structure, the formal authority system, and the primary work group. For example, if the subordinates' tasks are unstructured, they may experience confusion and role ambiguity, so that they are unclear how to perform well so as to attain their goals. In such circumstances, instrumental leadership, which clarifies what is expected of subordinates and how the task can be accomplished, is likely to be most appropriate. Where the task is well structured, such an approach is unhelpful. A leader who tries to structure and direct is likely to come unstuck. Subordinates are likely to feel dissatisfied or indignant at the unnecessary interference. Similarly, if the primary work group gives an individual ample social support, a supportive leader will not be particularly valued by that person.

To summarize, the leader has to take account of both the individual needs and characteristics of subordinates and the nature of the work environment. Given these factors, the leader needs to choose an appropriate style so as to influence the subordinates' motivation to perform the work.

The evidence

Most of the research on the path–goal theory has concentrated on instrumental and supportive leader behaviour, rather than on the other two categories which are participative and achievement oriented. Among the outcome measures which have been investigated are job satisfaction and subordinate performance.

The results of studies examining the model have been mixed. An early study by Dessler and Valenzi (1977) found that among workers performing structured tasks in a manufacturing company, instrumental leadership and worker satisfaction were positively correlated. For those workers performing less routine work, there was no effect of instrumental leadership. This evidence is the exact opposite of the predictions of path–goal theory. It predicts that those doing unstructured tasks will prefer instrumental leadership while those doing structured, routine tasks will not. More recent studies have also failed to support the contention that task structure will moderate the effects of instrumental leadership on job satisfaction (Keller, 1989; Schriesheim and Schriesheim, 1980). On the other hand, an investigation by Schriesheim and DeNisi (1981) in a bank and a manufacturing company, found that non-routine and unstructured tasks *did* moderate the effects of instrumental leadership on subordinate satisfaction, as path–goal theory predicts.

Perhaps the best single source of evidence for the path–goal theory comes from a meta-analysis by Indvik (1986). As mentioned in

Chapter 2, meta-analysis pools the results of a large number of separate research studies, so that the conclusions can be based on sample sizes of thousands, not the 50 or 70 of a typical individual study. In the case of Indvik, she analysed 48 different path–goal studies. The results support path–goal theory in part.

Indvik showed that when task structure is low, instrumental leadership is associated with greater subordinate satisfaction, satisfaction with the leader and intrinsic motivation compared with when the task structure is higher. This supports the theory. As far as subordinate performance is concerned, instrumental leadership is unrelated to performance, which is inconsistent with the theory. She also showed that supportive leadership does enhance satisfaction and performance in highly structured work settings, as predicted, though the strength of the effect on satisfaction was low. Similarly, when the task is unstructured, participative leadership enhances job satisfaction.

Problems with the path–goal theory

There are a number of problems with path–goal theory.

1   Many of the problems are the same as those of the Ohio State studies. There is the problem of *inconsistent findings*, the ignoring of the *informal group*, the *averaging* of measures of leaders' behaviours and problems of *measuring* the leaders' behaviours. The theory does consider situational factors, though, which were absent from the Ohio State studies.

2   As with the Ohio studies and other theories, there is the problem of *causality*. Do different leader behaviours cause differences in subordinate satisfaction and performance, or vice versa? Many of the studies testing the theory have been cross-sectional rather than longitudinal, so it is impossible to tell. One study, a longitudinal investigation of path–goal theory by Greene (1979), does throw light on this question. It showed that leadership behaviour did cause different levels of satisfaction among subordinates. If task structure was low, instrumental leadership led to higher work satisfaction. If task structure was high, supportive leadership led to higher satisfaction. But with performance the results were different. When task structure was medium or high, subordinate performance led to different levels of instrumental leadership. It seemed as if subordinate performance caused a leader to behave in a particular way rather than the other way round.

3   So much of the theory remains *untested*. Although the theory describes four leadership behaviour patterns and puts forward a number of contingent variables, most of the research has centred on the two dimensions of instrumental and supportive leadership, and only on task structure as a moderating variable.

4   There seems to be a difference in the findings according to whether *satisfaction or performance* is chosen as the dependent variable. The research evidence tends to support the theory when satisfaction is the outcome variable, but not when it is performance. This is disappointing when the theory's main interest is in predicting a subordinate's motivation to work hard and perform well.

5   Bryman (1992) concludes his evaluation with a useful summary of the theory's problems:

> the early promise of path–goal theory seems to be abating. The discrepant findings, the problem of causality, and the failure of the theory to predict performance in many studies are not encouraging. Further, the plethora of leadership styles and situational factors that the theory and research have put forward do not provide leaders with any clear guidance as to how they should behave, even if the findings were less inconsistent (p. 20).

SUMMARY

All contingency approaches attempt to answer the question of when one type of leadership style or approach is more appropriate than another. As we have seen in this chapter, the effectiveness of leader behaviours depends on the context in which it is placed. We have also seen that different theories or models stress different contextual variables or factors. No one contingency theory or model stands out as somehow 'better' than another. Whilst each of the contingency theories has some advantages and merit, they all have problems. It is therefore difficult to state a clear advantage for one over another. What is certain is that whatever the style or behaviour of a leader, it is the relationship which exists between the leader and follower and how each perceives the actions of the other that is important. This has been a major concern of attribution theorists, which is the next topic to which we turn.

4 Attribution theory of leadership

As we have seen throughout this book, the relationship which exists between leaders and subordinates and managers and employees can play an important role in determining the performance and satisfaction of all of the individuals involved in the relationship. Equally important, however, is how both parties perceive the actions of the other and to what they attribute those actions. Attribution theory suggests that any event can have a variety of causes. This gives rise to the idea that we all act as 'naive psychologists' in trying to create some order out of the abundance of possibilities which are presented to us in our lives. So attribution theory can be defined as the manner in which people try to discover cause-and-effect relationships in the events which occur around them. This attribution process is crucial to leader–follower and employer–employee relations.

In this chapter we will look at how attributions are made, the effects that can arise from them and how attribution theory can be applied to leadership. In doing so, we will examine attribution theory originally put forward by Heider (1958) and extended by Kelley (1967) with the principle of co-variation. We will also look at attributional models of leadership developed by Mitchell and Wood (1979) and examine some of the evidence obtained from research studies into this area. From this we will see that whilst attributions can sometimes be made accurately, the attributions of leaders and subordinates are often at considerable variance and sometimes quite inappropriate to the circumstances. They are also subject to many different influences and can be responsible for many adverse effects in an organization.

THE STUDY OF ATTRIBUTIONS

Attribution theory suggests that we observe the behaviour of others and then attribute causes to it. Initially put forward by Heider (1958), attribution theory focuses on the inferences that are used to deduce someone else's disposition or traits, from observations of their behaviour. Central to Heider's theory is the proposal that people see behaviour as being caused either by the individual in question (i.e. dispositional), or by the environment (situational). It makes a distinction between internal and external causes – that is, whether people initiate actions themselves, or purely react to the environment in which the action takes place.

To illustrate the attribution process and its importance let us take the example of a shop assistant who argues with a customer in front of yourself and other customers. The assistant shouts and threatens the customer in seemingly uncontrollable anger. After witnessing this incident, you might conclude that the assistant is bad tempered, rude and lacks self-control and perhaps should not be serving people. You may decide not to use that particular shop again. In fact this type of attribution is quite likely.

Research shows that people do have a strong tendency to attribute others' actions to internal, dispositional factors when evidence to the contrary is lacking. There could be other possible explanations for the scene described above. You could, for example, conclude that the assistant has previously been threatened by the customer and is simply responding to some earlier incident which you had not witnessed. In this case, you would be explaining the assistant's actions in terms of external, situational causes.

In situations like this and in many others, the conclusions you reach in making an internal or external attribution to explain behaviour can have important consequences. If you decide that someone has acted in the way they have because of internal causes and believe that it is due to their personality or nature, then you will most likely expect them to still behave like this on future occasions and this would influence your future dealings with them. However, on the other hand, if you decide that they have acted as they did because of external or situational reasons and are not normally like that, this would have an entirely different effect on you. The question is: how do we decide what type of attribution to make?

KELLEY'S CO-VARIATION MODEL

Kelley's Co-variation Model (1967) extends the work of Heider and attempts to explain exactly how we make judgements about internal and external causes. The principle of co-variation states that 'an effect is attributed to one of its possible causes, with which over time, it co-varies' (Kelley, 1967). That is to say that if two events repeatedly occur together, we are more likely to infer that they are causally related than if they very rarely occur together. Kelley's model suggests that if the behaviour to be explained is thought of as an effect of something which has occurred, the cause can be one of three kinds. The extent to which the behaviour co-varies with each of these three kinds of possible cause is what we actually base our attribution upon.

Kelley believes that in an effort to determine whether another person has acted in the way they did because of internal or external causes, first we should consider the extent to which others also behave in the same manner; this is known as Consensus. Second, we should consider the extent to which this person acts in the same manner at other times; this is known as Consistency. Finally, we should consider the extent to which this person behaves in the same manner in other contexts; this is Distinctiveness. Information about these three factors is then combined and forms the basis for our decision about the causes of the other person's behaviour.

To illustrate co-variation, imagine the situation if we see a person in a restaurant complain about the food, about the waiter and about the décor but in a situation where nobody else complains about these things. We would most likely conclude that the person was difficult to please and that the causation was internal. If, on the other hand, other people did complain (consensus is high), the same person had also complained in the same restaurant before (consistency is high) but we knew that they did not usually complain in other settings (distinctiveness is high), then we would perhaps instead infer that the person's behaviour stemmed from external causes and that the restaurant was at fault (see Figure 4.1).

Whilst there is some support for the co-variation model and evidence that people do use these means in assessing causation, there are also qualifications which need to be made. One popular criticism is that Kelley seems to have over-estimated people's ability to assess co-variation and gives an idealized view of how people come to draw

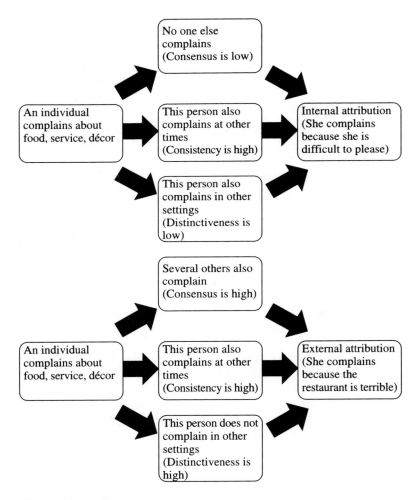

Figure 4.1 Attribution
Source: Baron and Greenberg (1990).

inferences about behaviour. The actual procedures which people adopt when inferring causality, imply that we are not as logical, rational and systematic as the model would suggest. There is also research which reveals that we frequently fail to apply the criteria correctly or sufficiently and thereby make errors in attribution.

Although we shall not investigate these aspects and errors any further in this chapter, the interested reader can explore some of these by referring to Jones and Nisbett (1971), Ross (1977) and Nisbett and Ross (1985).

ATTRIBUTIONAL PROCESSES BY LEADERS

Attribution theory can be applied to leadership. The attribution theory of leadership suggests that a leader's judgement about his or her employees' actions are influenced by the leader's attribution of the causes of the employees' performance. That is to say, leaders observe the performance of their followers and then try to understand why the followers' behaviour either met, exceeded or failed to meet, the leader's expectations. The leader's attributions of employees' behaviour then determines how the leader responds, just as much as does the actual behaviour itself.

Once an attribution has been made as to the cause of an employee's behaviour, the manager or leader then selects actions to deal with the behaviour. Thus, if a leader attributes a subordinate's poor performance to internal factors such as low effort or a lack of ability, he or she may reprimand, dismiss, or provide training for the employee concerned. If, however, poor performance is attributed to external factors such as a lack of material, or to work overload, the leader would need to concentrate on these factors and improve the situation instead of giving negative feedback to the employee.

The importance of leaders' causal attributions is emphasized in a survey carried out on 500 firms by Stoeberl and Schneiderjans (1981). They found that 97 per cent of the supervisors surveyed reported having problems in disciplining subordinates. The manner in which supervisors respond to ineffective subordinates is known to have a direct effect on group performance. If inappropriate measures are taken, substandard performance may persist and spread to other group members.

Mitchell and Wood (1979) have developed an attributional model of leadership which attempts to link leaders' actions to employees' poor performance (see Figure 4.2). By referring to this model we can see that it shows the connection and relationship between the components of employers' observations, information cues (i.e. distinctiveness, consistency and consensus, which were referred to earlier), causal attributions (that is, to what the leader attributes the

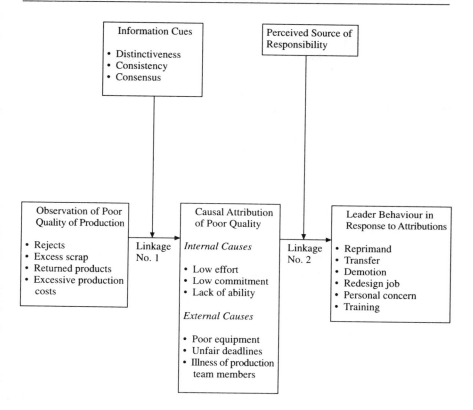

Figure 4.2 An attributional leadership model
Source: Adapted from Mitchell and Wood (1979).

problem), the perceived source of responsibility and, finally, the response that the leader makes.

Green and Mitchell (1979) have developed a two-stage model describing the manner in which supervisors respond to poorly performing subordinates. In the first step of the process, the leader diagnoses the cause of the employee's ineffective performance using Kelley's (1967) co-variation principle. Leaders analyse the subordinate's behaviour with regard to its consistency over time, distinctiveness across settings and consensus across employees. They then attribute the poor performance to factors that are either internal or external to the subordinate. In the second step of the model, leaders implement a corrective response to improve the performance. Green and Mitchell predict that leaders will select more punitive, corrective actions when poor performance is attributed to factors internal to the subordinate. This is in fact what is found, as we shall see when we consider the evidence obtained from studies of leaders' attributions.

It has been suggested by some researchers that the models of attributions are 'cold' models of information processing which assume that leaders and managers are rational and influenced only by objective data in the work environment. However, such assumptions are inconsistent with research which has investigated the effects of subjective influences on cognitive judgements. Zajonc (1980) for example, has reviewed studies which show that liking occurs early in the interaction with a stimulus and may affect cognitive processes to a significant degree. The 'likeableness' of subordinates will be discussed in greater detail later in this chapter (see pp. 54–5), but it is easy to see from this that if faulty attributions are made by leaders and managers because of other influences, then subsequent action taken might be totally inappropriate to the circumstances. This can easily lead to resentment and dissatisfaction amongst subordinates and result in substandard performance.

THE EVIDENCE

Research into the attribution theory of leadership is still in its infancy but there is evidence to reveal the types of attributions made by leaders and managers and the effects that these can have. Most of this research tends to relate to leaders' responses to subordinates' poor performance.

In what is perhaps the best-known study, Mitchell and Wood (1980) presented nursing supervisors with brief accounts of errors committed by nurses. The accounts suggested that the errors arose either from lack of effort or ability (i.e. internal causes) or from an over-demanding work environment (i.e. external causes). Supervisors were asked to state what action they would take in each case. Results showed that the supervisors were more likely to direct action at the nurses themselves when they perceived the causes as internal and at the environment when causes appeared to be external. This does suggest that attributions by leaders can, sometimes, be made quite accurately and the appropriate action taken.

Considerable research, however, reveals that leaders and subordinates differ in their perceptions of the causes of poor performance by employees. Mitchell and Wood (1980) and Ilgen *et al.* (1981), for example, both found that leaders generally tend to make internal attributions. That is, they tend to blame subordinates for poor performance, whereas subordinates themselves tend to make external attributions by blaming environmental factors.

There is also evidence that, if a subordinate has a poor previous work history, the likelihood of an internal attribution is greater. The previous poor work history makes it more likely that the employee will be blamed for the current poor performance rather than other factors. If the effects of the poor performance are serious or harmful, then internal attributions are even more likely. However, if subordinates make excuses or apologise for their poor performance, the leader is less likely to make internal attributions (Wood and Mitchell, 1981).

Green and Liden (1980) found that once a leader has made an internal attribution of a subordinate's poor performance, the leader's response to this is more likely to be to impose punitive measures and closer supervision. This is as predicted by Green and Mitchell (1979) and was also found by Mitchell and Wood (1980). The nature and severity of the response is then influenced by the subordinate's previous work history, whether the effects are serious and whether an apology is proffered (Ilgen *et al.*, 1981).

Ilgen *et al.* (1981) found that a leader's rating of a subordinate who performs poorly is also affected by a number of other factors. They established, for example, that if the leader's own rewards are affected by the subordinate's poor performance, then the leader is likely to respond more favourably, to rate more highly and to implement further training. This again suggests a bias, albeit one which operates in favour of the employee.

DO MANAGERS FAVOUR CERTAIN SUBORDINATES?

Are managers and leaders fair to subordinates whom they dislike or who differ by means of other characteristics? Common sense tells us that one of the things most likely to affect the types of attributions made by leaders and supervisors and the subsequent action taken is the consideration of whether the supervisor likes the other person or not. Perhaps surprisingly, the question of like and dislike is not always found to have an effect on the actual attribution process but this may be due to a number of factors. However, liking or not liking does consistently have an effect on the corrective action taken after subordinate poor performance. This was the finding in a two-part study carried out by Dobbins and Russell (1986a).

In the first part of this study, Dobbins and Russell presented a vignette describing an incident of poor performance, committed by either a liked or disliked subordinate, to 96 undergraduate subjects. The 'leaders' (subjects) made attributions for the appropriateness of a series of corrective actions. It was found that the subordinate likeableness did not affect leaders' attributions of the cause of the poor performance but it did have a bearing on the corrective action taken. Specifically, leaders were more inclined to punish and conduct performance counselling and less inclined to support a disliked subordinate than they were a liked subordinate.

Obviously, there are limitations in conducting a study in an experimental setting. In order to overcome this, a second part of Dobbins and Russell's study was carried out in a field setting using 98 managers from an assortment of industries. They were asked to describe an actual incident of poor performance and the action they had taken. They were also asked to respond to the same attribution process and corrective action items that were used in the first study. It was found that leaders were more inclined to attribute poor performance to internal factors when the subordinate was disliked, than when he or she was liked. In relation to the corrective action taken, the findings of the first study were replicated with leaders again responding more negatively towards disliked subordinates. These findings are supported by those of Turban et al. (1990) who found that a supervisor's liking for a subordinate positively influences the treatment of the subordinate and also evaluations of the subordinate's work performance.

Dobbins and Russell believe that the inconsistent findings between the two parts of their study, in relation to the actual attributions made, may be explained by the ambiguity of the cause of the poor performance. When the cause of poor performance is ambiguous, due to multiple factors being present or the available information being inconsistent, leaders draw on other information such as their liking or disliking of the subordinate concerned in order to make the necessary attribution. This bias has been taken further by Dobbins (1986) who investigated differences between male and female leaders' responses to poorly performing subordinates. Dobbins found that the corrective actions of female leaders were more affected by 'likeableness' and the sex of the subordinate than were the corrective actions of male leaders.

Dobbins and Russell suggest that since multiple interpretations of behaviour are invariably present in an actual work setting, leaders' attributions will almost always be based on likeableness. If this is the case, then clearly the most appropriate action may not always be selected. If poor performance is permitted when a subordinate is liked but not when he or she is disliked, feelings of inequality may emerge, not only in the 'aggrieved' subordinate but also amongst other employees. These may result in resentment, dissatisfaction and persistence of poor performance, leading possibly to absenteeism, theft and even sabotage. The potential for this to cause harm in any organization is obviously enormous. Figure 4.3 illustrates the different types of action taken based on liking and the negative outcomes which can arise from this.

EMPLOYEES ALSO MAKE ATTRIBUTIONS

Attribution is a two-way process, of course. Employees, too, attribute causes to their leaders' behaviours as well as to their own and view the leader as having an effect on their (the employees') performance. They also develop either positive or negative attitudes about the leader. When employees are successful, they tend to rate their leader as successful. When they are not, they tend to blame the leader and distance themselves from him or her. In poorly performing football teams, for example, it is usually the manager who gets fired, not the players.

Dobbins and Russell (1986b) have investigated the self-serving biases in leaders' and subordinates' attributions for group performance. The findings revealed that leaders attributed low group performance to subordinates, whereas subordinates attributed low group performance to leaders. Clearly each group prefers to see the other as responsible for poor group performance, whatever the real causes may be.

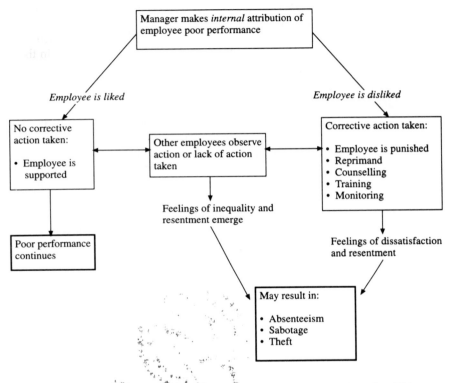

Figure 4.3 The effects of a manager's corrective actions based on liking a subordinate
Source: Based on Dobbins and Russell (1986a).

SUMMARY

It becomes obvious from the evidence that the attributions made by individuals are complex and affected by many factors. It seems likely from the evidence that a subordinate or employee whose success or failure at work is attributed to environmental factors will have a very different relationship with his or her leader than will an employee whose similar success or failure has been attributed to personal factors. In the one case, the employee will be content with his or her employment whilst continuing to perform poorly. In the other case, the employee is likely to feel frustration and resentment at the way he or she has been treated. Clearly leaders need to be diligent in attributing causes and selecting options to deal with employee performance problems. Effective leadership lies just as much in recognizing the perceptions of the parties involved, as it does in the reality of what actually takes place.

5   Do leaders make a difference?

Leaders, as we all know of course, are important ... or are they? Throughout this book we have looked at different leadership styles and have seen that these can, and often do, have a major effect on subordinates and followers. Yet nearly all of us will at some time or other have observed a group, or been part of a group, where the leader has had little or no effect. In addition, probably one of the most disappointing aspects of research on leader behaviours is that no strong, consistent relationships between particular leader behaviours and organizational effectiveness, has ever been found (Howell *et al.*, 1990). Suddenly, doubts begin to arise. Perhaps leaders and managers might not be necessary after all. Could it be that the objectives of a group might still be met without them?

One suggestion for the lack of effect which leaders sometimes have on organizations concerns the leaders' own characteristics and personality. They are sometimes too weak and inexperienced, or just not suited to the position they hold. Another possibility is that sometimes other factors may substitute for a leader's influence, making the leader superfluous. The questions then become more specific. Are subordinates able to manage their own work and behaviour? Can followers develop norms to control and direct themselves? Or is it something in the structure of the work itself which makes the presence of a leader unnecessary?

The questions posed above have been addressed in research aimed at examining the need for leadership, the romanticization which surrounds leadership and the substitutes which might replace leadership. In this chapter we will examine some of this research and some of the misconceptions which surround leadership. We will look in particular at the need for a reinvention of leadership advocated by Meindl (1992), the romance of leadership described by Meindl and Ehrlich (1987) and substitutes for leadership proposed by Kerr and Jermier (1978). We will also look at some of the criticisms made of these theories.

THE CASE FOR A NEW APPROACH

In a radical and controversial approach to the question of leadership and its effects, Meindl (1992) calls into question the value of continuing to research leadership using conventional wisdom and argues for a new approach to be used. The emergence of leadership has long been recognized by researchers as an important process (e.g. Bass, 1954; Bavelas et al., 1965). However, Meindl believes that leadership emergence studies have been concerned in the main with understanding who emerges as leaders. The focus has been on who the leader is and what the leader does, in a leader-centred research agenda. Subordinates and followers are the ultimate targets of such studies but leaders are most definitely the object. Meindl suggests that as an alternative to this convention it is possible to define followers as objects and the leaders as targets. He points out that conventional approaches tend to be located at the leader end of the 'who' and 'what' in leadership studies. This tends to provide a too narrow account of the real significance of leadership. Meindl argues the case for a need for the *reinvention of leadership* from a radical social psychological point of view which would instead be located in the follower end of the 'who, what' argument.

In Meindl's view, the emergence of leadership depends heavily on the followers. Leadership emerges as a state of mind within the follower, or an experience that he or she undergoes. Without the experience of being in a state of leadership, followership would not exist and leaders would not emerge. Leaders are only important in so far as they may eventually become the targets of the followers' thought systems. Meindl believes that in this type of approach, leadership becomes the 'emergence of an ideology', a development in a group of a particular way of thinking about their relationships to one another and their relationships to the tasks they carry out.

THE ROMANTICIZATION OF LEADERSHIP

This argument is taken further by Meindl and Ehrlich (1987), who suggest that people have a strong tendency to romanticize leadership. They perceive it as more important than it really is and link leadership more closely to performance than is warranted. They believe that over the years the concept of leadership has become firmly engrained into collective efforts to understand and improve organizations. They point out that survey results indicate that most academics agree that leadership is the most important topic of all within the realm of organizational behaviour (Rahim, 1981). Although there have been misgivings, questions and differing opinions about the subject, the commitment and investment in the concept of leadership has resulted in it becoming almost sanctified over the years, leading to a romanticized concept of leadership.

They suggest that in order to come to terms with and understand the causes, nature and consequences of organizational activities and the myriad of interactions that create and maintain them, people need to translate them into simple human terms that they can understand and communicate easily to others. For this reason, people make attributions about cause and effect. From this attributional process, the concept of leadership has come to represent and convey a sense of understanding and control over different problems that require explanation and responsive action. Meindl and Ehrlich have extended this attributional analysis of leadership further by suggesting that as an explanatory concept, leadership has now acquired a special status, not merely an alternative to other equal explanations but a 'heroic, larger-than-life value all of its own'.

One of the key rationales behind the recent interest in attributional processes associated with leadership, is that people may react to similar outcomes very differently depending on the particular causal inferences they make regarding these outcomes (see Chapter 4). The general argument is that the way in which something is explained in part determines reactions to it. Meindl and Ehrlich suggest that the possibility that differences in causal interpretations can alter broad subjective evaluations of events and outcomes can be used to demonstrate the value and significance placed on the concept of leadership.

Meindl and Ehrlich have reasoned that the degree to which a particular causal factor affected subsequent reactions to organizational events would to some extent reflect the intrinsic significance and value of that factor. In this way, it is possible that this value can be powerful enough to influence the evaluation of the outcome to which it is attached.

It is well known that people tend to value causal factors associated with desirable effects positively, if for no other reason than their usefulness as a means to an end. An example of this would be supporters attributing a team's winning streak to its leadership by the captain, in a situation where perhaps the players didn't appear to be playing too well. This, however, can also operate in reverse so that in some cases the desirability or value of a cause (i.e. in this case leadership) which is thought to produce an effect (i.e. the team's success) determines the value of that effect or outcome – that is to say, exactly how successful the team are actually seen to be.

Meindl and Ehrlich believe that the value and significance

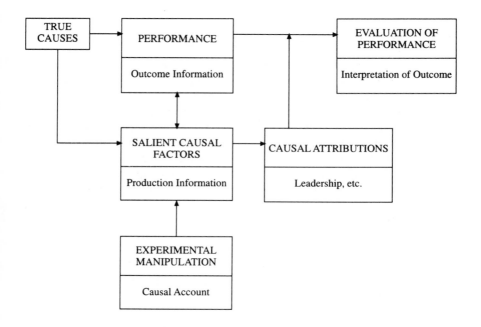

Figure 5.1 Working model of leadership outcomes
Source: Adapted from Meindl and Ehrlich (1987).

ascribed to leadership as a causal force tend to enhance the subjective value of its believed or presumed effects in relation to the outcome of performance in any group or organization. To make this clearer: in the example given of a winning football team, this would mean that the value attributed to its brilliant captaincy (if that is what the success had been attributed to) could make the team's success seem even greater than it really is. This, then, would explain why other supporters who did not view the captaincy as quite so brilliant might also not see the team as doing quite so well.

Given the suggestions for people's romanticization of leadership, Meindl and Ehrlich believe that people faced with causal accounts attributing outcomes to leadership will evaluate those outcomes more favourably than when the same performance outcomes are attributed to factors not directly associated with leadership. They have proposed a working model which can be used to operationalize this process and which shows the connection between the various stages involved in the process (see Figure 5.1).

THE EVIDENCE FOR ROMANTICIZATION

In order to test the suggestion that people have a strong tendency to 'romanticize' leadership, Meindl and Ehrlich presented 111 students on a Master of Business Administration programme with information about an imaginary firm. This information included a five-year summary of selected indicators of the firm's performance which consisted of total sales, profit margins, net earnings and stock price. Attached to the data was a paragraph describing the firm's key operating strengths. The content of this paragraph was varied, so that each of four groups of subjects received a different version of the operating strengths. These different versions attributed the firms performance to:

- its top level management team;
- the quality of its employees;
- the changing patterns of consumer needs and preferences; or
- federal regulatory policies.

After reading one of the versions of key operating strengths and other information, subjects were asked to rate two aspects of the firm's overall performance, its profitability and its risks. The results

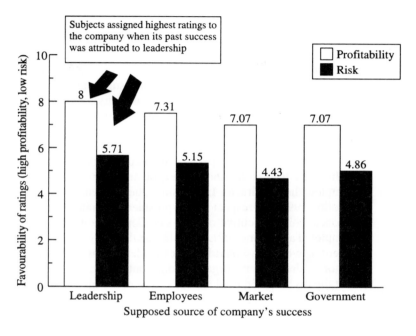

Figure 5.2 Leadership: evidence that we overestimate its importance
Source: Based on Greenberg and Baron (1993).

obtained showed that the students rated the firm more favourably when its performance was attributed to the top management than when it was attributed to any of the other factors. This suggests that the imaginary company was rated as more profitable and lower in risk when it was believed that this good performance was due to leadership factors than when it was due to any of the other factors. This seems to confirm the view of Meindl and Ehrlich that people have a tendency to romanticize leadership and over-emphasize its importance and its effect on outcome (see Figure 5.2).

The results from the study described above tend to complement findings from previous research by Meindl *et al.* (1985). The earlier study had shown that people have a bias towards viewing leadership as a causal force when they account for organizational performance under ambiguous conditions, when the underlying causes are impossible to determine. It appears that they attach a value and significance to leadership as an explanatory concept. Meindl *et al.* believe that although it is difficult to specify how this value is transmitted, their results suggest that something akin to a powerful 'halo' characterizes leadership as an explanatory concept, so that anything connected with the concept tends to take on a similar value and significance.

Going further still, Meindl (1989) has suggested that the comparatively recent preoccupation with transformational leadership, and with charisma in particular, is indicative of what he calls 'hyper-romanticization'. By this, he suggests that in the recent writings on the New Leadership, charismatic and transformational leadership have been accorded an especially inflated significance.

In order to test the above idea, business students were asked to complete the Multifactor Leadership Questionnaire (MLQ) (Bass and Avolio, 1990) in respect of ex-president Ronald Reagan and Lee Iacocca, chief executive of Chrysler Corporation. The students also completed a Romance of Leadership Scale (RLS) which measures the extent to which an individual sees leadership as a highly significant factor in determining organizational outcomes. The results showed that the higher an individual's RLS score, the more likely he, or she, was to see Reagan and Iacocca as transformational leaders.

In another similar study, Ehrlich *et al.* (1990) investigated how subordinates perceived the manager of a high technology defence contracting company. This manager had been generally accredited with being responsible for a radical transformation in the company's fortunes in recent years. The MLQ and RLS, together with a measure of recording extra effort, were administered to employees of the company. The results showed that the manager emerged with high scores on charisma and also individualized consideration (see Chapter 9). The correlation between charisma and the Romance of Leadership Scale was fairly high (0.32), although non-significant.

The value of this study is not so much in the correlation between charisma and the romance of leadership but in relation to how attributions of charisma are made. It was found that employees who knew the particular manager well, and had dealings with him directly, were less likely to describe him as charismatic than were the others. This finding suggests that the separation of subordinates from leaders may contribute to the perception of the leader as charismatic, which helps to perpetuate the romanticization of leadership. A distant or rarely seen leader can attract an aura which often disappears on closer and more regular contact.

It can also be shown that 'performance cues' (factors which prompt and explain performance), can be applied to the domain of charismatic leadership and thus contribute towards romanticization. Previous studies have consistently shown that ratings of leadership behaviours are susceptible to performance cues. Pillai and Meindl (1991) have extended these earlier findings to show that evidence of a 'crisis', followed by good performance attributed to a leader, can heighten ratings of charismatic leadership more than does just good performance alone. In this study, Pillai and Meindl read subjects' different versions of a case about a fast food company, describing the industry, the performance of the company over the last ten years and a profile of the chief executive officer (CEO). Descriptions provided to the subjects varied only in terms of information relating to the company performance patterns. These performance patterns were manipulated by varying two factors, positive or negative growth and the presence or absence of a crisis. In all versions, the profile of the CEO was unchanged.

The results revealed that in the cases of a crisis followed by recovery, perceptions of charismatic leadership appeared to peak, whereas in the cases of crisis followed by decline, perceptions of charismatic leadership reached a nadir. These findings suggest that crisis, combined with good performance, can add to a leader's stature. This helps to perpetuate the effect that we have seen, namely the romanticization and glamorization of leadership.

CRITICISMS OF ROMANTICIZATION

As might be expected in respect of any new and controversial theory, the description and explanation of romanticization has not gone unchallenged. Bass (1990) in particular has criticized the general approach. He believes that it goes too far in the opposite direction by relegating leadership to a very minor role in human affairs. Bass argues that even a cursory glance at military, political and business history would suggest that the effects of leadership are real and not, as implied by Meindl, all in the mind. Yukl (1989) also believes that Meindl considers leadership to be unimportant and has attempted to trivialize it.

Bryman (1992) points out that Meindl's examination of charisma and romanticization could be turned on its head by the suggestion that charisma is, and always has been, in the eyes of the follower. In defence of his proposals, Meindl argues that his is not a challenge to leadership *per se* but is a consciousness-raising endeavour to have leadership seen in a different light.

Meindl himself points out that there are, of necessity, limitations in the studies he has carried out. These relate to the use of rather coarse and one-sided themes designed to eliminate different attributions from the subjects in a contrived laboratory setting. It is reasonably safe to assume that the themes used would never occur in real settings in the pure forms used in studies. Real accounts in a real setting are likely to be far more complex and centred on different issues entirely. Meindl emphasizes that awareness of such issues should temper the interpretation of his results. He suggests that future studies might benefit from examining processes in real ongoing events, using individuals with a vested interest in the organizations studied.

It does seem that people have a tendency to romanticize leadership. Possibly leaders and managers are not quite as crucial as previously thought. That is not to suggest that they are usually and normally unimportant. On the contrary, leaders and managers can, and often do, play a key role in groups and organizations. What is suggested is that their necessity should never be taken for granted. On occasions, other factors might substitute for them.

SUBSTITUTES FOR LEADERSHIP

As pointed out at the beginning of this chapter, Howell *et al.* (1990) note that one of the most disappointing aspects of research on leader behaviours is that no strong, consistent relationship between particular leader behaviours and organizational effectiveness has ever been found. What all of the previous research has in common, though, is a conviction that hierarchical leadership is always important. Even situational approaches to leadership share the assumption that although different situations require different leadership styles, in every situation there is some type of leadership style which will always be effective. Despite this, it has been shown in numerous studies that circumstances often counteract the potential power of leadership, making it virtually impossible in some situations for leaders to have much impact regardless of their style, or how good the fit is between the leader and the situation.

The approach to leadership which is least dependent upon the assumption that hierarchical leadership is always important, is the path–goal theory (see Chapter 3). Under circumstances when goals and paths to goals may be clear, House and Mitchell (1974) point out that attempts by the leader to clarify paths and goals will be both redundant and also seen by subordinates as imposing unnecessarily close control. House and Mitchell believe that although this style of control may increase performance by preventing malingering, it can also result in decreased subordinate satisfaction.

A further premise, originally made by House and Mitchell (1974), is that even leader behaviours which are unnecessary and redundant will still have some impact on subordinate satisfaction, morale, motivation performance and acceptance of the leader. This presents the seemingly paradoxical situation, that while leader attempts to clarify paths and goals are recognized by path–goal theory to be unnecessary and redundant in certain situations, in no situation are they explicitly thought to be totally and completely irrelevant.

In order to resolve this dilemma of the occasional successes, but also frequent failures, of the various theories and models of leadership, Kerr and Jermier (1978) have developed a framework for conceptualizing the many situational variables which can have an effect on a leader's influence. They believe that a wide variety of individual, task and organizational characteristics have been found to influence positively the relationships between leader behaviours and subordinate satisfaction, morale and performance. However, other factors and variables have the effect of acting as substitutes for leadership. The substitutes neutralize its effects by tending to negate the leader's ability to either improve or impair subordinate satisfaction and performance.

Individual, task and organizational characteristics can all have an effect on leadership behaviours in different ways. When individuals have extensive experience or training, little supervision is necessary because they already have the knowledge, skills and expertise to know what to do and how to do it. Professionals such as doctors, lawyers and scientists often do not need or want much supervision. Characteristics of the task can also make leadership less necessary. When tasks are simple or repetitive, or provide feedback on how well the job is being carried out, leaders do not need to provide much instruction or feedback themselves. If the task is interesting or enjoyable, subordinates may be motivated by the work itself so as to make supervision less necessary. In organizations with detailed

Table 5.1 Substitutes and neutralizers for leadership

Variable		Task-oriented leadership	People-oriented leadership
Organization variables:	Group cohesiveness	Substitutes for	Substitutes for
	Formalization	Substitutes for	No effect on
	Inflexibility	Neutralizes	No effect on
	Low positional power	Neutralizes	Neutralizes
	Physical separation	Neutralizes	Neutralizes
Task characteristics:	Highly structured task	Substitutes for	No effect on
	Automatic feedback	Substitutes for	No effect on
	Intrinsic satisfaction	No effect on	Substitutes for
Group characteristics:	Professionalism	Substitutes for	Substitutes for
	Training/Experience	Substitutes for	No effect on
	Low value of rewards	Neutralizes	Neutralizes

written procedures, regulations and rules, little direction is needed by employees once the policies of the organization have been learned.

Table 5.1 shows a total of 11 situational variables of either the individual, the task or the organization that can tend to substitute for, or neutralize, leadership behaviours. The table also shows the effect that the presence of a particular variable can have on both task oriented and people oriented leadership by acting either as a substitute for, or neutralizing, leadership. A 'substitute' for leadership operates by making the leadership style unnecessary or redundant whilst a 'neutralizer' counteracts the leadership style and prevents the leader from displaying certain behaviours. Other researchers have also identified what they term 'enhancers' which have the effect of amplifying a leader's impact on employees (Howell *et al.*, 1986). These are all moderator variables, since they have the effect of moderating the influence of a leader.

To explain the notion of substitutes and neutralizers further, we can consider the example of positional power. Where this is low, perhaps because the leader is physically separated from subordinates, the leader's ability to give directions to subordinates is greatly reduced. This has the effect of neutralizing the influence of the leader in both a task oriented and people oriented style of leadership. Other variables, such as high group cohesiveness or professionalism, can also substitute for leadership and make it redundant or unnecessary.

Group cohesiveness and professionalism can both be particularly strong substitutes. A work group comprising a closely knit team of experienced and highly trained individuals can often negate a leader's directive influence. Howell *et al.* (1990) believe that this is particularly evident in 'the white heat of danger, when the whole system threatens to collapse'. The stress involved creates a need for competence amongst those present in the situation and can often involve ignoring orders from leaders who are not present in the 'front line'. This can be illustrated by the example of emergency and paramedic teams who invariably operate on their own initiative and without direction.

The value of Kerr and Jermier's framework is that it can help a leader to tailor his or her leadership style and adapt it to complement the organizational situation. For example, the work of a bank clerk provides a high level of formalization, with highly structured tasks and little flexibility. There would be little point in this situation in adopting a task oriented style, as the organization itself already provides structure and direction. Instead, a people oriented style might be best. On the other hand, in police organizations, where there is generally very strong cohesiveness but great uncertainty in the situations which arise, it may be that a task oriented leadership approach is more appropriate. The value is in adapting a style which ensures that both task needs and people needs are met.

THE EVIDENCE FOR SUBSTITUTES

A number of studies have provided support for the assertion that many different variables can substitute for leadership. Kerr and Jermier (1978) conducted two field studies using police officers from a large city force and a university police force. Police organizations provide ideal settings to test the importance of leader substitutes, since formal rank and command control are essential elements of the structure. If important leader substitutes are found in these settings, their presence can be reasonably assumed in other organizations. Data for these studies were gathered using a 55-item substitutes for leadership questionnaire and also various leader behaviour–subordinate outcome measures.

The findings revealed a number of significant differences between the two forces. The city police saw themselves as more formalized and less rule-inflexible than did the university police. University police showed greater indifference towards organizational rewards and perceived their supervisors to be more spatially distant. Despite the differences, it was possible to identify a large number of task and group characteristics and organizational variables which either substituted for, or neutralized, leadership behaviours. These substitutes and neutralizers acted by reducing the impact of leader behaviours upon subordinate attitudes and performance. However, an important distinction was established between them. Substitutes provide a person or thing to act in place of the formal leader's influence. Neutralizers do not. The effect of neutralizers therefore is to leave an 'influence vacuum'.

In most organizations, substitutes exist for some leader activities but not for others. Effective leadership can perhaps best be described as being the ability to supply subordinates with needed guidance and satisfactions which are not supplied by other sources. The essence of Kerr and Jermier's work is that leadership is only one factor in successful work-group performance.

Some other studies have also helped to confirm the existence of substitutes and neutralizers. For example, a study by Sheridan *et al.* (1984) investigated nurses' job performance, as rated by their supervisors. Job performance was more strongly affected by factors which could serve as substitutes for leadership, such as the nurses' education, group cohesiveness and the technology available, than it was by their supervisors' leadership style or behaviour. These moderators tended to substitute for the head nurse's leadership, whereas the hospital's administrative climate appeared to neutralize it.

Williams *et al.* (1988) have raised the issue of the lack of construct validity of Kerr and Jermier's Substitutes for Leadership Scale. Their own work has improved the reliability and integrity of the original scales. However, they suggest that some problems still exist with the construct validity of some of the subscales. However, on the positive side, they quote evidence regarding the independence of the subscales. Those that were found to be highly inter-correlated, made sense from a conceptual point of view. They also note that the scales are relatively free of social desirability bias.

Yukl (1994) points out that although available studies provide some support for some of the propositions of leader substitutes theory, the theory has so far not been adequately tested and not enough is known about specific substitutes and neutralizers. He notes a number of weaknesses in the theory and the research. These relate to matters such as the direction of causality, the difficulty in identifying specific substitutes and neutralizers and the question of appropriate statistical procedures for testing the theory. Despite these problems, Yukl believes that a positive contribution of the theory has been to focus more attention on conditions that serve as substitutes and also in providing a more balanced approach for understanding how group performance can be improved.

SUMMARY

What can we conclude on the issue of the romanticization of leadership and on leader substitutes? It does seem that people have a tendency to romanticize leadership and over-emphasize its importance. Certainly there also appears to be some moderator variables which can have the effect of sometimes neutralizing leadership and sometimes actually substituting for it. All of this might lead to the conclusion that leadership is completely unimportant and that from now on we can manage without it. However, this is not what is being argued. None of the researchers whose work has been described are suggesting that leaders are superfluous and totally redundant. What they are saying is that leadership should not be taken for granted and that other factors might on occasions act as moderators for it and have an effect on its outcome and effectiveness.

6 Power and influence

It is impossible to talk of leadership without also discussing the question of power and influence. The term 'leadership' denotes that the leader usually has some sort of power over those he or she leads, although a person with power is not always necessarily the leader. A leader may decide to give power away, or encourage others to empower themselves, as we will see in Chapter 10. Or the power may come from attributions of charisma. Without some degree of power, a leader or manager would have difficulty influencing or controlling those he or she leads.

Even when it is not given away, power still does not always only reside exclusively in leaders and managers. Often lower-level employees, followers or subordinates, may exercise considerable power as well. Power can be wielded by controlling the flow of work or withholding support or information from a manager or leader. In addition, expert power can enable lower-level employees to influence those who are hierarchically senior to them. To some extent each person in a group or organization can possess some sort of power under certain circumstances.

Power can also often be found in people by virtue of the positions they occupy in society and the respect they are given by others because of those positions. This may be so even though the legitimate power they possess might be restricted to certain circumstances and conditions. Examples of this are the roles of doctor, clergyman, schoolmaster or police officer, although many feel that the influence associated with these positions has diminished in recent years. Clearly then, power is not an all or nothing affair but may change from circumstance to circumstance.

In this chapter we shall look first at the definition and nature of power and the circumstances under which it may arise and operate. We will then look at the different types of power and the way in which these can be used. We will also consider some of the evidence obtained from research studies into the effectiveness of the different power bases. Finally we will look at the need that some people have for power and also how power pervades through an organization. In doing so, we will look in particular at the Bases of Individual Power developed by French and Raven (1959), the Uses of Power outlined by Yukl (1989) and also the description by McClelland (1971, 1985) of the Need for Power and Achievement.

DEFINITION AND NATURE OF POWER

There are many definitions of power. One useful definition is: 'the potential ability of a person or group to influence another person or group'. Note in this definition the importance of the pivotal term 'potential'. A person or group may be able to influence others but may choose not to exercise that potential. Another important term used in this definition is the word 'influence'. It is important to distinguish influence from the notion of power, as the two terms do not mean the same thing. Vecchio (1991) suggests that 'influence' tends to be broader, subtler and more general than 'power'. Whilst both influence and power have the capacity to change the behaviour of others, power does so with some regularity and authority, whereas influence is weaker and less reliable.

Although there is a subtle difference between power and influence, there is also a clear relationship. If a person or group of people affects another in such a way that it causes a change in their opinion or behaviour, then they can be said to have influenced the other and thereby exercised power over·them. Another way to describe this relationship is to consider that power has the capacity to influence, whilst influence itself is a measurement of an amount of power.

The term 'power' can be used in referring to any number of individuals, groups or organizations, but more than one person or entity must always be involved for the concept to apply. Power cannot be used in social isolation as it is a social term which expresses interactions between people. Hellriegel *et al.* (1992) suggest that power is also never absolute or unchanging but is a dynamic relationship which changes as individuals and situations change. Attempting to understand power relationships therefore makes it necessary for us to specify and understand both the situation in which it occurs and also the individuals involved in that situation.

Researchers have examined the means people use to influence each other and exercise power. Yukl and Falbe (1990) for example have identified a number of different tactics of social influence which are used in social settings. These range from simple consultation to the tactic of exchange by promising benefits in return for complying with requests.

BASES OF INDIVIDUAL POWER

In any organization, the distribution of power is often unequal, although in the case of co-operatives, as we will see later, they do try to have equal power. Under normal circumstances, however, some individuals have a greater capacity and also opportunity to influence people successfully than do others. This of course raises the question of what sources of power people have at their disposal and from where does that power emanate.

The most widely used and recognized analysis of the basis of individual power is the classic framework developed by French and Raven (1959). This work identifies five general sources of power that

Table 6.1 Individuals' power: five major bases

Type of power	Description of base
Reward power	Based on the ability to control valued organizational rewards and resources (e.g. pay and information)
Coercive power	Based on control over various punishments (e.g. suspensions and formal reprimands)
Legitimate power	Based on the belief that an individual has the recognized authority to control others by virtue of his or her organizational position (e.g. the person is a high-ranking corporate official)
Referent power	Based on subordinates liking the power-holder (e.g. the superior is friends with a subordinate)
Expert power	Based on the accepted belief that the individual has a valued skill or ability (e.g. expert medical skills)

Source: Based on French and Raven (1959).

stem from the individual characteristics of people and also from the type of relationships which exist between those people with power and those with less. These bases are described as legitimate power, reward power, coercive power, expert power and referent power. A brief summary of these bases of power are shown in Table 6.1.

Legitimate power

This type of power is essentially the same as authority and is vested in a person by virtue of their position in the hierarchy of any organization. It is the recognized right of individuals to exercise authority over others purely because of their position. Usually legitimate power is derived from the individual's rank or position.

In police work, custody officers, who are normally the rank of sergeant, are given legitimate power by law to refuse the access of any officer of any rank, even senior to themselves, to any prisoner in their care if it appears likely that it would contravene the guidelines for the care and well-being of the prisoner. In all other respects, the sergeant would normally be subject to the power and authority of those senior in rank. Legitimate power does not always rest at the top of a hierarchy.

The fact that legitimate power stems from a person's position or rank in an organization also does not mean that the higher ranking person can control all aspects of a subordinate's behaviour. Managers, and others in authority, only have authority over those aspects that are recognized and accepted as being under their area of responsibility. For example, although a typist may recognize the authority of his or her boss to have them type office correspondence, they may well refuse to type the personal letters of the boss's family, or to run errands.

If we look at the effectiveness of legitimate power, we see that it can only be effective if it is accepted by the people it is meant to control. The key point is that legitimate power applies only to the range of behaviours which are recognized and accepted by the parties involved. If people withdraw their support and acceptance of legitimate power, then that power can cease. *Coups d'état*, revolutions and strikes are examples of this.

The degree or extent of legitimate power also varies from organization to organization. In highly disciplined organizations, such as the police and armed forces, the power inherent in each rank is clearly specified and strictly followed. In organizations such as laboratories and universities, which favour more individualistic effort, the layers of power are usually less well defined.

Reward power

This is the power which individuals have by virtue of their control over resources which are of value to others. The most obvious examples of this in an organization are the rewards of pay, promotion and preferred work assignments. The rewards given do not have to be material in nature but can consist of the offering of status, praise or acknowledgement. Allowing access to the director's dining room or admission to a select group are examples of this type of reward power. Thus, the person who is in control of rewards and resources can wield considerable power irrespective of additional bases of power.

However, a manager or leader should always beware of rating more highly the attraction to others, of things which he or she values. For example, although a leader may value highly financial rewards and promotion, others may not. If a reward is not valued by the potential recipient, then this form of power is ineffective. When a subordinate does not want promotion and has other sources of income, then the manager's reward power may be diminished and other forms of reward may need to be found. Many managers find themselves in this position, particularly with older employees nearing retirement.

A leader or manager must also be in control of rewards in order to be able to operate this form of power. In cases where a union controls pay and job assignments and promotion is based more on seniority, then reward power will be ineffective.

Reward power can give managers a distinct advantage in obtaining desired outcomes from those they manage, if the conditions are right. However, Handy (1993) argues that reward power is not usually popular. People do not like to be reminded that they can in effect be bought. Sometimes rewards are grudgingly accepted by employees, even though they may be sought out of necessity.

Coercive power

This form of power can also be described as physical power or the power of superior force. It is the power which exists when someone has the ability to punish or harm, either psychologically or physically, another person. The threat of punishment can be a strong means of invoking compliance from someone. To the extent that subordinates try to avoid such punishment, a manager can be said to have coercive power over them.

At its mildest, coercive power can take a subtle form such as criticism or denial of support or friendship. At its extreme, it can take the form of actual physical control by force, as is the case when it is used in prisons and mental hospitals. In a working environment it usually refers to punishments such as demotion, salary cuts, dismissal, suspension or the removal of expenses or other advantages. In order to be effective, coercive power does not necessarily have to be used. Its existence, or even belief in its existence, can be sufficient. Many researchers point to the fact that punishments are only effective if used properly. Vecchio (1991) in particular believes that the application of coercive power requires good social judgement. He points out that a manager must on occasions be expected to take firm action, such as when a subordinate is unproductive or hinders productivity. However, if the manager is too harsh or indiscriminately inflicts punishment on all employees, then morale and productivity are likely to suffer.

Despite its potentially negative effects, coercive power is frequently used in most organizations. It underlies much of the routine compliance which takes place in relation to timekeeping and meeting deadlines. The fear of being fired, ridiculed or reprimanded can be a potent incentive to comply.

Expert power

Expert power is the power vested in someone because of their acknowledged expertise in a particular area. Most people readily seek and accept the advice of experts. The credence given to doctors, lawyers and other similar professionals are examples of the acceptance of expert power. Few people resent being influenced by those they regard as experts and for this reason expert power is often regarded as the least obnoxious or objectionable of the power bases.

As expert power is the most socially acceptable source of power, it is also the most sought after. But it can sometimes give rise to dubious claims of expertise. Specialist departments or individuals will have their advice accepted by the organization only as long as their expertise is recognized and accepted. Expert power is given by those over whom it will be used.

Handy (1993) notes that expert power is comparative. A person is an expert for only as long as he or she knows more than anyone else present in that situation. Once someone else arrives with even the smallest degree of further expertise, then the first will lose most, if not all, of their power. As he says, 'in the country of the blind, the one eyed man is king – that is until he with two eyes comes along'.

Referent power

This is the power that a person has by virtue of possessing qualities which are admired by others. It arises from the desire to identify with the qualities of attractive people and to be like them. In this respect it usually surfaces as imitation and in many ways is also similar to the concept of charisma (see Chapter 8). Whilst referent power is often associated with well-known figures such as political leaders, film stars and sports personalities, it also applies to managers and other individuals in an organization who are admired because of their personalities and ability. Colonel 'H' Jones, who was killed during the Falklands War, was said to have been a man of great charisma with so much referent power that his men would willingly follow him anywhere.

OTHER BASES OF POWER

It has been questioned by some researchers whether there really are only five bases of power. Yukl and Falbe (1991) suggest that although the five bases described by French and Raven clearly exist, there may be three more – information power, persuasive power and charisma.

Yukl and Falbe believe that the eight bases of power reflect two underlying power dimensions (see Figure 6.1). They describe the first of these underlying dimensions as *position power*, which reflects the power derived from a person's formal position in an organization. This comprises legitimate, reward and coercive power together with their newly included information power. This latter power base relates to the extent to which a supervisor provides the information needed to do the job. The other dimension Yukl and Falbe describe as *personal power*, which comprises expert and referent power, together with the newly identified persuasive power and charisma. These two new dimensions refer to the power exercised by virtue of the supervisor's qualities and characteristics.

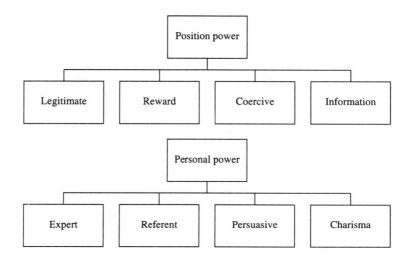

Figure 6.1 The relationship between underlying power dimensions and their relevant power bases
Source: Based on Yukl and Falbe (1991).

THE EVIDENCE

Now that we have looked at the different individual bases of power the obvious question is, is one type of power base more effective than another? A large number of experimental and field studies have been carried out to examine this question. Podsakoff and Schriesheim (1985) have reviewed a number of these studies and reanalysed much of the literature. They note that although the results from several of the studies are inconsistent, in the main, reward power, legitimate power and coercive power, all tend to be either negatively related, or unrelated, to performance and subordinate satisfaction. That is to say that increases in the levels of those bases of power tend either to have no effect on employee performance or to be associated with decreases in performance and satisfaction.

Expert and referent power, on the other hand, tend to be positively related to performance and also to satisfaction with supervision. This suggests that subordinates tend to be motivated by expert and referent power and so perform more effectively and are more satisfied with their supervision. Expert power and referent power tend to show a negative correlation with employee withdrawal behaviour. The greater the levels of expert and referent power used, the less the absences from work and the less the turnover of subordinates. This trend is not found in relation to reward, legitimate and coercive power. Similar results tend to be found with employees' intentions to leave their organizations. The greater the levels of expert and referent power used, the less likely employees are to state future intentions to leave the organization.

Subordinates also consistently report that expert power and legitimate power are the strongest reasons for them complying with supervisors' requests. Referent power is given as a less important reason while reward power and coercive power are the least important reasons why employees do as they are requested.

These findings suggest that expert power and referent power might be the most effective bases of power for supervisors to use and that reward, legitimate and coercive power are not as effective. This view of the evidence is supported by Yukl (1994).

CRITICISMS OF THE RESEARCH

The main criticism is that most of the studies included in the review have used self-report questionnaires to measure the use of power bases and their effect on subordinates. Self-report questionnaires are notoriously subject to the effects of social desirability and attributional bias – that is, the need that most of us have for social approval and acceptance by others that our behaviour is appropriate and acceptable. Probably most employees would not admit that they do what their supervisor requests primarily to receive greater pay-offs or to avoid being punished. Subordinates are more likely to say that they comply with supervisors' requests because the supervisor is an expert in his or her field, or because he or she is a kind or pleasant person. Podsakoff and Schriesheim (1985) believe that these biases may have distorted the results of many studies.

Other criticisms are that the research results fail to take into account the interdependency of the different power bases, whereby one type of power affects the use of another. Also, supervisors respond differently to different types of subordinate characteristics and behaviours. So the results may underestimate the variability of supervisors' behaviour.

Podsakoff and Schriesheim believe that whilst research so far might reflect the desirability of expert and referent power, much of the research in this area has been undertaken without much apparent concern for either the validity or reliability of the measures used.

A final point concerns the question of cause and effect. None of the studies included in the review allow us to infer that the use of a particular power base has *caused* the effects observed. It cannot be concluded that the use of expert power, for example, causes better subordinate performance or less absence from work, only that the different variables correlate.

OTHER EVIDENCE

Since the review carried out by Podsakoff and Schriesheim, further studies have examined the use of French and Raven's bases of power. Perhaps the most notable of these is the study by Yukl and Falbe (1991) mentioned earlier, which examined a larger variety of power sources and also the underlying dimensions of position power and personal power. This study also examined the use of lateral power as well as downward power. One hundred and ninety-five subordinates and 220 peers of 49 middle and lower level managers were interviewed and questioned in three large companies connected with pharmaceuticals, chemicals and financial services. The objective was to increase knowledge of the types of power commonly used in organizations to influence subordinates and peers. Respondents were asked to rate the importance of eight types of power as reasons for being influenced to do things requested by the managers.

One of the further power bases used by Yukl and Falbe in this particular study, was that of persuasiveness. Persuasiveness, legitimate power and expert power were the most important reasons given for employees complying with peer and supervisor requests. This is in agreement with the studies reviewed by Podsakoff and Schriesheim, but it is in contrast with other studies where legitimate power was found not to be as important as referent and expert power.

The results obtained by Yukl and Falbe, show that legitimate power is a very important source of day-to-day influence in organizations. They believe that the reason for this is that authority is more acceptable and easier to use than most forms of power as the basis for influencing people to fulfil regular expectations in a reliable manner. It can also be used without incurring the costs associated with other forms of power. The findings are consistent with the proposition made by other researchers that authority systems are essential for large organizations to function smoothly and efficiently. However, the results also generally support prior findings that personal power (comprising of expert and referent power and also charisma) is more important than position power as a source of leader influence on subordinate performance.

This now presents the paradox that, on the one hand, legitimate power and authority are recognized as being the most effective power sources in ensuring compliance but, on the other hand, expert and referent power and charisma also are. So, the question now is: where does all of this leave us and which really is the most effective source of power? To explain this paradox, Yukl and Falbe suggest that the sources of power which are important for obtaining commitment to unusual requests appear to be different from the sources which are important for obtaining compliance with routine requests.

The implication from this is that both legitimate and coercive power may be important for the day-to-day routine running of organizations and for the control and direction of subordinates in normal circumstances. However, expert and referent power may be the most effective for matters over and above the normal daily running of organizations and for matters which require some sort of commitment to the organization and to the individual who leads it.

THE USES OF POWER

It is important to realize that the sources of power which have been identified don't necessarily operate independently and a manager may possess and use varying amounts of each. Effective leaders probably use a mixture of different types of power. The use of one power base can also affect the strength of another. For example a person can gain greater legitimate power by being promoted to a higher position and so have a greater capacity to operate reward power in respect of pay and conditions. However, at the same time by also exercising more coercive power and thereby becoming unpopular, the same person may lose some of their referent power. In effect, the way in which a manager or leader uses one type of power can either enhance or limit the effectiveness of power from another source.

A study by Greene and Podsakoff (1981) emphasizes this point. The study examined the relationship between different power sources in two papers mills. One of the mills changed an existing incentive pay plan based on employees' performance to one which was based purely on seniority. The other mill retained the original pay performance incentive. It was found that in the first mill, employees' perceptions of supervisors' use of reward power was lowered, whilst perceptions of coercive power were increased. Perceived use of referent and legitimate power also decreased whilst expert power appeared to remain the same. Perceptions of the use of power at the second mill, which had not changed the pay performance incentive, remained the same. These results show that the interpersonal sources of power that influence behaviour are both complex and interrelated.

It has been discussed earlier that many of the research studies carried out have used self-report questionnaires to measure the power base used by leaders. This has in effect meant simply asking those with power, what power they use. The method has been criticized by some researchers who question whether this is an accurate way of measuring power because of the subjective bias which invariably affects this type of measurement. A questionnaire developed by Hinkin and Schriesheim (1989) has overcome many of the problems and is now seen as an accepted means of measuring power. Box 6.1 shows examples of the types of questions asked with an explanation of how these are completed and scored.

OUTCOMES FROM USES OF POWER

It becomes clear from the evidence that power can be wielded in many different ways. Yukl and Taber (1983) have presented a number of general guidelines for the use of power and the outcomes which potentially result when a leader tries to exercise power. These outcomes which they describe as commitment, compliance and resistance, all depend on the leader's base of power, how that base is operationalized and the individual characteristics of and relationships with the subordinate concerned.

The outcome of *commitment* is likely if workers accept and identify with their leader and share the leader's point of view. Employees with commitment will be highly motivated by requests that seem important to the leader and will enthusiastically carry out instructions. A committed worker will often work just as hard as the leader. As we have seen from the evidence reviewed above, expert and referent power and also charisma are the sources most likely to generate commitment in followers or subordinates.

Compliance means that an employee will obey orders and carry out the leader's instructions but only because it is necessary to do so in order to remain in employment. Employees will often not be enthusiastic about their work and may disagree with instructions but will carry them out because they are obliged to. Many interactions between bosses and subordinates come into this category and are more likely to be the result of legitimate and reward power.

Resistance occurs when workers deliberately try to avoid carrying out instructions and fight against the leader's wishes or orders. They may deliberately neglect a project in order to ensure that it is not done

BOX 6.1 MEASURING THE DIFFERENT POWER BASES USED BY SUPERVISORS

Employees completing this scale are asked to rate how closely various prepared statements describe their own supervisor's power behaviours. This is done by giving a score to each question to indicate how strongly they agree or disagree with the statement. Scores range from 1 = strongly disagree, to 5 = strongly agree. Typical questions are:

'My supervisor is able to . . .

1 influence my pay level;
2 make my working conditions difficult;
3 explain my work tasks to me;
4 share his/her experience with me;
5 help me to feel important.'

(Note that these are only samples of the type of questions used and are not a complete range.)

Four items measure each of the five different bases of power. By collecting a number of different measurements for a particular supervisor it is possible to gauge the degree to which the supervisor is recognized by others as using each type of power.

Source: Based on Hinkin and Schriesheim (1989).

in the way a leader wants. This is often a reaction to coercive power.

The approach to management and the use of power has, in most organizations, traditionally been autocratic, with supervisors in the main wielding power by virtue of their superior position in an organization's hierarchy. This often takes the form of legitimate and coercive power as in the above example. Employees comply through fear of the loss of employment and the rewards which go with it. More recently, however, there is a trend in business environments towards a process of *empowerment* (see Chapter 10). This involves putting employees in charge of what they do and of the decisions which are made, thereby making them more responsible for getting things done.

Empowerment has the effect of making everyone in an organization feel more in control and hence encourages more contribution to organizational goals and objectives. The process relies more on communication than command, with supervisors acting more as consultants who provide the means for the work to be carried out. In this type of system, executives no longer hoard power and the five bases of power described by French and Raven are largely diminished. Participation groups and consultation groups are a feature of many modern organizations.

Having seen the manner in which power can be used, the outcomes which can arise from exercising power and also the alternatives to the traditional approach to management, the question now arises of what makes some people seek power, whilst others are quite content to be led. In the next section we will look at the need that some people have for recognition and achievement and the parallel question of the need that some people have for power.

THE NEED FOR ACHIEVEMENT AND THE NEED FOR POWER

It appears quite obvious that with increased power comes increased levels of responsibility and with increased responsibility usually comes the added burden of worry and pressure. This raises the question of why some people seek power while others do not.

For example, consider the position of Members of Parliament and particularly Cabinet Ministers. Once they achieve office, they gain responsibility and the power to influence and direct the actions of others. However, with that position comes criticism for many of the actions they take or fail to take. They can become subjected to intrusion into their private life with the potential that this has for causing family problems and also embarrassment. Why, then, should it be that MPs seek and accept power and influence?

The work of McClelland (1971, 1985) throws some light on this question. McClelland's acquired needs theory proposes that certain types of needs are not present at birth but are acquired through life experiences. These acquired needs are the need for achievement, the need for affiliation and the need for power.

The *need for achievement* is characterized by the desire to accomplish something difficult, to attain high standards or to surpass others. McClelland believes that if children are encouraged to do things for themselves and receive reinforcement, they will acquire a need to achieve. Such people often tend to become entrepreneurs in later life.

If children are reinforced for forming close personal relationships and for avoiding conflict, they develop a *need for affiliation* and a need to establish warm relationships. These people tend to be 'integrators' who like to co-ordinate the work of others. Integrators usually have excellent people skills and are able to establish positive working relationships with others.

The *need for power* is associated with the desire to influence, control, be responsible for, or have authority over others. People with a strong need for power enjoy winning an argument, defeating an opponent, eliminating a rival or enemy, and directing the activities of a group. Such people usually seek out positions of authority (such as manager, public official, lawyer or police officer) in which they can exercise influence and direct the activities of others. In contrast, people with a weak need for power are unlikely to be assertive and may genuinely believe that it is wrong to tell others what to do. McClelland suggests that if children get satisfaction from controlling others, and are reinforced in this behaviour whilst young, they will often acquire a need for power in later life.

McClelland differentiates between different types of need for power and believes that a high need for power is expressed in different ways depending upon another trait called *activity inhibitor*. People with low activity inhibition are motivated to satisfy the need for power in selfish ways by dominating others and using power to satisfy their own hedonistic desires. People with high activity inhibition, on the other hand, have strong self-control and are motivated to satisfy the need for power in socially accepted ways. This latter motivation for power might describe the need for power of MPs, which gains expression as a desire to serve others and bring about change.

The need for power is related to the successful attainment of the higher levels of organizations, as a study by McClelland (1971) showed. Managers at an American company were studied for a period of 16 years. Those with a high need for power were more likely to follow a path of continued promotion to the higher levels of the company. Managers with a high need for achievement, but low need for power, tended to peak earlier in their careers and at lower levels. McClelland suggests that the reason for this is that achievement needs can be met through the task itself, whilst power needs can only be met by ascending to levels at which an individual has power over others.

McClelland and Burnham (1976) believe that maturity and effectiveness in power relationships is determined by selecting the appropriate form of power use. They studied groups of business managers and found that higher level managers generally tended to be high on power motivation but low on affiliation motivation. They had a particularly strong desire to exercise power but less need to be liked by people. Those with a high affiliation motivation but low power motivation, tended not to reach the higher levels of organizations. McClelland's acquired needs theory and a needs-oriented approach have not gone unquestioned. For example, Mischel (1973) and Mitchell (1979) query the very existence of needs and whether any attention at all should be paid to them. Despite these criticisms, the work of McClelland does present one of the most comprehensive and influential explanations to date of why some people seek and accept power.

SUMMARY

We have seen in this chapter how power can be derived from a number of different sources and can be used effectively in a variety of ways. It has been stressed that power is not an all-or-nothing affair but can vary from situation to situation and is dependent on who is present in any situation. We have also seen the outcomes which can ensue when a leader exercises power and some of the reasons why people feel the need to achieve power. One question which must arise in the minds of many readers is whether having too much power, or being 'power-crazy' might be a bad thing. Most readers will recognize that there is an almost overwhelming ambition in some people to succeed and to achieve power and domination in whatever they do. Successful businessmen such as Rupert Murdoch, Tiny Rowlands and the late Robert Maxwell are examples of this. It is likely that these all have (or had) high levels of power motivation. Whilst normal ambition is admirable, problems arise when the need for power over others becomes an end in itself. Mulder (1977) believes that some people have an addiction to power where the striving for success can become an overriding dominant passion. It is not hard to see that this can lead to a leader's downfall. It is to leader failure that we turn next.

7 *Leaders who derail*

Much of this book has implicitly been about success. It has examined questions such as, what is this thing called leadership, what makes managers and leaders different, and do leaders make a difference to organizations and subordinates? It has been about existing or potential leaders and what it is that they do that makes them successful. So it is about time that we turned our attention to the question of how and why people hold on to positions of power and responsibility and who fails and why. A term sometimes used to describe this failure to hold on to leadership is *derailment.*

DERAILMENT

Derailment is a vivid and useful phrase. It conveys the sense that previously successful individuals can find themselves leaving the rails and being throw off track in ways that they did not wish. It is not that they have shunted themselves off onto a siding or into the engine-shed of retirement. The end of the line happens to all of us at some stage. As Studs Terkel (1974) has noted, jokingly, all careers pass through five stages depicted by the lines:

'Who is this guy, John Fortune?'
'Gee, it would be great if we could get that guy, what's his name?'
'If we could only get John Fortune.'
'I'd like to get a young John Fortune.'
'Who's John Fortune?'

Rather, derailment is an involuntary leaving of the main line, through events such as sacking, redundancy, being transferred, opting for early retirement, being sidelined into 'special projects', or 'plateaued' without any chance of further advancement. These events take place not as a result of a manager's own wish or at a time of his or her own choosing.

It was work at the Center for Creative Leadership (CCL) in Greensboro, USA, by McCall and Lombardo (1983), which first used the term derailment extensively. The original study involved interviews with 80 male top executives and human resource managers in large corporations. The study was later followed up by a study of 76 women executives. There were four main aims of the research:

1   Why were derailed executives successful in the first place?
2   What were the 'fatal flaws' that led to derailing?
3   What events surfaced those flaws?
4   How did those who derailed differ from those who made it to the top?

The term 'successful' was defined as:

Reached one of the 10–20 top positions in the corporation, or had lived up to his full potential as the organization saw it.

The term 'derailed' was defined as:

Achieved a very high level, but did not go as high as the organization had expected. May have been plateaued, demoted or fired, accepted early retirement, or had responsibilities reduced.

THE DERAILERS AND THE ARRIVERS

The results showed that the successful individuals, those who made it to the top, possessed a number of desirable characteristics. They were intelligent and ambitious people, with strong technical skills, who worked hard and were prepared to make sacrifices. They were identified early and subsequently had outstanding track records. In these respects the successful, and those who *had* been successful but had become derailed, were remarkably similar. What was different about the two groups was interpersonal skill. The most common reason for derailment was insensitivity. The derailers were much more often abrasive, cold, aloof, arrogant or intimidating. The 'arrivers' (individuals who continued to be successful) were more skilled at dealing with others, were diplomatic and avoided confrontations whenever possible. Seventy-five per cent of arrivers were described as having a special ability with people, compared to just 25 per cent of the derailed. This failure to get on with others was particularly noticeable in the male derailers, rather than the female ones. Other reasons for derailment were overmanaging (an inability to delegate or empower others), ruthless over-ambition (leaving a trail of bruised people) or an inability to be strategic (dealing with tactics, the nitty-gritty, the 'how' rather than the 'what' of long-term strategy).

Every manager researched by McCall and Lombardo had both strengths and weaknesses. None of the successful executives had all the strengths and none of the derailers had all the weaknesses. Sometimes derailment seemed to be just bad luck, being in the wrong place at the wrong time. These managers were the victims of a downturn in economic conditions, or a major decline in business performance, or political battles over which they had no control. However, a later CCL study with the same broad objectives extended the work and identified six factors as contributing to derailment (Lombardo and Eichinger, 1989). These traits and skills are as follows:

1 Poor treatment of others, involving: over-ambition; over-independence, isolation; abrasiveness, lack of caring; volatility and unpredictability under pressure.
2 Difficulty in building a team, involving: poor selection; being dictatorial or over-controlling; not resolving conflict within the team; poor delegation.
3 Difficulty in being strategic, involving: continuing to do, rather than seeing that things get done; inability to deal with complexity and ambiguity; collapsing under pressure of a new situation.
4 Lack of follow-through, involving: poor attention to detail; disorganization; not completing things; letting others down, untrustworthiness.
5 Over-dependence, involving: sheltering under same boss or mentor for too long; over-reliance on others to shield weak spot; relying too much on one strength.
6 Poor relationships with senior managers, involving: inability to persuade; inability to adapt to boss with different style; disagreements about strategy; inability to influence across functions.

Table 7.1 The process of derailment

Success at 30	Latent problems/ untested areas at 30	Changing demands	How things look at 40
1 Independent, likes to do it alone	(a) Doesn't develop subordinates (b) Doesn't resolve conflict among subordinates (c) Poor delegator (d) Has never chosen or built a staff	Team-building, staffing, developing	Can't mould staff
2 Controlling, results-oriented, single-minded	(a) Has trouble starting new jobs (b) Gets irritated easily when things don't go right (c) Doesn't develop a strategic perspective (d) Has never made a transition to an unknown area	Giving up old ways of doing things essential to succeed at more complex assignments	Can't make transitions
3 Creative, conceptually strong	(a) Lack of attention to detail (b) Disorganization (c) Speedboats along; leaves people dangling (d) Hasn't really completed an assignment in depth	Depth, awareness of how one is perceived if one doesn't follow through well on commitments or details	Lacks follow through, i.e. can't be trusted to perform
4 Brilliant driver, ambitious, high standards	(a) Overly ambitious, bruises others (b) Needs no one else (c) Abrasive (d) Lacks composure (e) Has not learned how to get the most out of people	Building and mending relationships, stability required for trust	Poor treatment of others

5 Has a single notable characteristic, e.g. lots of energy, raw talent or a long-term mentor	(a) Too many eggs in one basket (b) Staying with same person too long (c) Hasn't stood alone	Increasing complexity requires broader skills and repertoire, standing on one's own without a shield (e.g. talent or supportive boss)	Overdependence on a single strength
6 Contentious, loves to argue, takes strong stands	(a) Doesn't know how to sell a position or to cajole (b) Has to win (c) Has trouble adapting to those with different styles (d) Not learning how to lose gracefully or to influence those over whom one has no control	Cajoling, persuading, understanding the interpersonal process	Strategic differences with upper management, can't influence across functions

Source: Adapted from Michael M. Lombardo, Center for Creative Leadership, Greensboro, 1988.

The derailment research is intriguing in the way it emphasizes that it is the failure to adapt that is a major contributor to derailment. What is a useful trait and a predictor of success at an early stage in a manager's career can easily turn out to be the seeds of failure at a later point. Strengths become weaknesses. Events conspire. Blind spots start to matter. Changes brought about by a new boss, a radically different job, a reorganization, or entry into the upper echelons of the hierarchy, mean that the successful manager must change and adapt to remain successful. Derailers often have the same formative experiences as those who arrive, but fail to learn from them. They miss the meaning. They continue to rely on previous successful behaviour, or they have personal traits which are 'fatal flaws' that block learning.

Take the example of the most common reason for derailment, insensitivity. This flaw was tolerated when the individual was a lower-level manager, particularly if the manager was brilliant technically. Once at higher levels, the excellent technical skills were no compensation for insensitivity and abrasiveness. In addition, a manager's technical skills and expertise were usually greater than that of subordinates at lower levels, and a source of achievement. At higher levels the strength could become a weakness if arrogance led to the manager ignoring advice and overmanaging subordinates who had greater technical knowledge.

Table 7.1 takes other examples of strengths becoming weaknesses. It illustrates the process of derailment and the demands brought about by changing circumstances.

Table 7.2 What major influences have helped you develop as a manager?

Rank order	Statements	Score out of 100	SD
1	Ability to work with a wide variety of people	78.4	16.4
2	Early overall responsibility for important tasks	74.8	18.0
3	A need to achieve results	74.8	21.6
4	Leadership experience early in career	73.6	22.8
5	Wide experience in many functions prior to age 35	67.6	23.6
6	An ability to do deals and negotiate	66.4	21.6
7	Willingness to take risks	62.8	21.6
8	Having more ideas than other colleagues	61.6	22.8
9	Being stretched by immediate bosses	60.4	26.0
10	An ability to change managerial style to suit occasion	58.8	24.4
11	A desire to seek new opportunities	56.8	25.6
12	Becoming visible to top management before age 30	56.0	26.4
13	Family support (wife/parents)	55.2	29.2
14	Having a sound technical training	54.8	26.0
15	Having a manager early in your career who acted as a model (from whom you learnt a lot)	52.0	27.6
16	Overseas managerial/work experience	41.2	30.0
17	Experience of leadership in armed forces (peacetime/wartime)	40.4	33.6
18	Having special 'off the job' management training	32.8	24.4

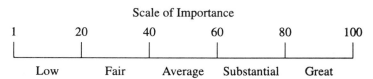

Scale of Importance

1   20   40   60   80   100

Low   Fair   Average Substantial Great

Source: Margerison (1980).

Some derailed managers were chameleon-like. Outwardly they could be charming, personable and warm when it suited them. At other times they could be argumentative, selfish and manipulative. Over a period of time, it became apparent that the manipulative side was their preferred side and they alienated too many people (Conger, 1990). In contrast, arrivers were sensitive, tactful and considerate, and were able to get on with a wide variety of people. When they disagreed with someone they said so, but tactfully, while the derailed managers were blunt and aggressive. Work by Margerison (1980) with 208 chief executives from top British companies supports the CCL findings. When asked what were the major influences which had helped them develop as a manager, the most important one cited by the chief executives was 'an ability to work with a wide variety of people' (see Table 7.2).

MANAGING THE MANAGERIAL TRANSITION

The topic of transitions and careers has been much researched in psychology (see Nicholson and West, 1988, for example). The transition from technical expert to manager and leader is one of the most difficult to manage in a person's career, but one of the most crucial for later success. Margerison (1980) illustrates this as a cross-over (see Figure 7.1). In the early stages of a person's career the job is often largely technical in nature. The technical skills may be checking accounts, selling knitwear, teaching French or operating a computer. After a while the demands change. You may still be checking the accounts or selling a product, but along come other responsibilities like supervising others, managing a team, or persuading colleagues. These tasks are more managerial in nature. You are slowly but surely removed more and more from the technical aspects of the work. The timing of the cross-over from largely technical to largely managerial differs from industry to industry and specialism to specialism. It also differs from country to country. Qualified people tend to leave university and other forms of higher education and training later in Germany and France, for example, than they do in Britain. So the cross-over date is likely to be later. Sometimes the change-over is signalled by a change in job title from, say, accounts clerk to accounts manager, or sales assistant to sales manager, though not always. From his survey of 208 chief executives in Britain, Margerison notes that in large UK corporations the cross-over takes

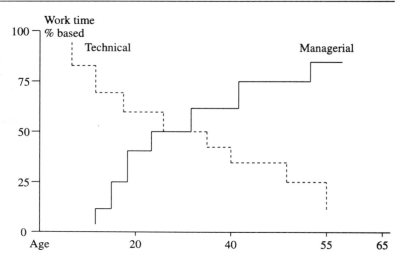

Figure 7.1 The managerial cross-over
Source: Margerison (1980).

place between the ages of 30 and 40. Whenever and however it happens, though, it is a critical period of adjustment. For some it is an exciting challenge, for others a trial.

The reason why it is a difficult and crucial period is that people are leaving what they know and what they are qualified to do by training and experience. They have been successful up to now for just that reason, they are good at the technical aspects of the job and have been rewarded for it. Now there is a step into the unknown. Yet it is always so tempting to go back. As soon as there is a crisis, colleagues are likely to invite you back into doing what they and you know that you are good at, even though now you should be coaching them to do it. 'We have a real problem with this key customer, Joe. You were always so good with her; you always sorted it out. Could you just spend some time with her? Please!' And back Joe goes, back to the tasks that he enjoyed so much, back to the thrill of 'real' problems and away from the difficulties of being strategic or managing others in the organization. Or you call yourself back. 'I'll fix this bug in the program, just this once. I know it's not my job any more, but it'll only take a minute. It'll be so much easier than instructing someone else. This is fun!'

So you can see why the transition is often so problematic. Teachers who enjoy teaching and contact with children become expected to do more administration; sales managers now sit in an office and manage others rather than burning up the miles on the motorway in the company car, flushed with the success of clinching yet another order. People who were at first rewarded for their excellent individual contributions are, later in their careers, expected to build a team, manage a network of others, see that things are done, rather than doing the task alone. The cross-over transition can happen in most jobs. One has to decide either to stay as a 'techie' or specialist, or else learn to leave the baggage of the past and move on to management and leadership.

BRITISH DERAILERS

The CCL study by Lombardo and colleagues was a milestone in derailment, but it was based on research with American managers. Do the same results apply in Britain? Broadly, the answer seems to be 'yes'.

A study at Cranfield School of Management (Tyson *et al.*, 1986) looked at 204 executives who had been made redundant and were attending outplacement counselling, designed to help them cope with redundancy and find another job. Each redundant manager took the 16PF, a well-known personality questionnaire. The profiles of the outplacement managers were compared with those from a group of employed managers. Compared with this group, the redundant managers were:

more: calm; socially bold and uninhibited; imaginative; unconventional.
less: shrewd (more natural and forthright); self-critical; tense, overwrought.

The Cranfield study concluded that it was those executives who lacked 'political' skills (the so-called 'N' factor on the 16PF) who were more likely to be made redundant compared to other executives. Both groups were alert, intelligent, independent, emotionally adjusted and with good leadership scores. The derailers just did not demonstrate cool realism and political sensitivity. A similar American study also used the 16PF with 49 redundant executives attending outplacement counselling, and found similar results (McLoughlin *et al.*, 1983). Although differences on the shrewd ('N') factor between redundant and employed managers did not reach statistical significance, it was in the same direction.

A second British study by Brindle (1992) found similar results regarding intelligence and independence, but without the difference in cool realism. Brindle studied the characteristics of 676 redundant managers using the 16PF and another well-known personality questionnaire, the Occupational Personality Questionnaire (OPQ). Eighty-five per cent of the sample were male. Derailment was measured as the amount of time managers had stayed with their last organization before being made redundant. Derailers, who stayed less time, were:

more: intellectual; conceptual; innovative; change oriented; independent; active; extroverted.
less: emotional and warm; conscientious; traditional.

The astute reader will have noted that the research reviewed above is in the trait approach tradition (see Chapter 2). There are, of course, organizational issues contributing to derailment. Moving people too quickly, without the proper training or experience, is a classic organizational mistake. It is known as the Peter Principle which states that there is a tendency for people to be promoted to their 'level of incompetence'. It's a mistake, too, to move people too slowly, so that they do not develop new skills and experiences, or to let one failure restrict progress, or to fail to provide effective and timely feedback on performance.

SUMMARY

The conclusions from the derailment studies seem to be these. First, intelligence does not protect you from being derailed. It does not distinguish derailers from arrivers and in one study seems positively associated with derailment. It's the *use* of intelligence that matters. If you have practical intelligence, such that you are aware of the politics and realities of organizational life and have the cool realism to do what is required to keep your nose clean, then you have a better chance than average of keeping your job. You need to be streetwise. It is a sad fact that the more imaginative, unconventional and independent-minded managers are less likely to stay the course. As the Cranfield researchers point out, the derailers were not organiza-

BOX 7.1 BREAKING THE RULES

Anita Roddick is the founder and managing director of Body Shop International. She opened her first shop in Britain in 1976 selling skin and hair preparations in specimen bottles that could be brought back for refilling. Her products combine originality with environmentally friendly methods and ingredients. In less than ten years her first shop had grown into a chain with franchises around the world. She attributes her success to 'energy, curiosity and breaking the rules'. In her book, *Body and Soul*, she writes:

'My instinctive trading values were diametrically opposed to the business practices of the cosmetics industry in just about every area:

- They were prepared to sell false hopes and unattainable dreams; I was not. From the start, we explained to customers in simple language everyone could understand exactly what a product would do and what it wouldn't do.
- They sold hype; I was so innocent I didn't even know what hype was.
- They thought that packaging was important; I thought it was totally irrelevant. We happily filled old lemonade bottles with our products if a customer asked.
- They tested on animals; I was repulsed by the practice and made it clear that I would never sell a product that had been tested on animals.
- They spent millions on market research; we simply said to our customers, 'Tell us what you want and we will try and get it for you.'
- They all had huge marketing departments; I never fully understood what marketing was.
- They had enormous advertising budgets; we have never spent a cent on advertising. At the beginning we couldn't afford it, and by the time we could afford it we had got to the point where I would be too embarrassed to do it.

Box 7.1 continued

> - They talked about beauty products; I banished the word 'beauty'.
> - They worshipped profits; we didn't. In all the time I have been in business we have never had a meeting to discuss profits – we wouldn't know how to do it.
> - Finally, and most importantly, they thought it was not the business of business to get involved in wider issues, in the protection of the environment or involvement with the community; I thought there was nothing more important.'
>
> *Source:* Anita Roddick, *Body and Soul*, London, Ebury Press, 1991.

tion men and women. They didn't seem to be as adept at playing the organization game. Of course, derailment refers to managers in organizations that they do not own. There are different rules if you are the founder of the company. Anita Roddick of Body Shop and Richard Branson of Virgin are just two who have made reputations and businesses from being unconventional (see Box 7.1).

Second, it helps to be self aware, especially as regards your ability to get along with others. Arrivers in just about all the studies were more interpersonally skilled. It is particularly important to have a good relationship with your boss. Survival skills at a time of redundancy may well include an ability to avoid unpopularity with senior managers. Social awareness and political skills may be difficult to learn without management development exercises aimed at providing feedback and skills training but they are vitally important.

Finally, there is some suggestion, notably from the CCL research, that failure to adapt to changing circumstances can lead to derailment. Of course, if you are politically astute, you may spot the changes before others. Yet knowing you should adapt and being able to do it are two different things. Kotter (1982) studied general managers and noted that all of the ones he researched knew how to adapt, but only the effective ones put their knowledge into practice. Once again, it comes down to practical, applied intelligence.

8 *Charismatic leadership*

Throughout history there have been men and women who we would call charismatic. They have inspired organizations, religious groups, even whole nations, to follow them even to death. Martin Luther King, John F. Kennedy, Winston Churchill, Adolf Hitler, Alexander the Great (see Box 8.1) are just some of the names that spring to mind. For a long while, though, it was only psychologists and other social scientists who studied religious movements and political leadership who were concerned with charisma. However, the concept explored in the 1940s by the sociologist, Max Weber, has come back in favour and is now much researched by psychologists interested in organizational leadership.

Charismatic leadership has been defined as the capacity to 'make ordinary people do extraordinary things in the face of adversity' (Conger, 1991). The word 'charisma' means 'divinely inspired gift' in Greek. There has been a debate in the literature, though, about whether the charisma is mainly the possession of certain traits (similar to the great man, great woman theory in Chapter 2), or the result of situational conditions (such as organizational crises) or an interaction between leaders and their followers. Most people now agree that it is best viewed as an interaction, a special type of relationship that exists between leader and followers. Charisma is seen as the result of specific reactions of followers influenced by leader characteristics and behaviour in a particular situation. So Hitler's charisma, to take a 'dark side' example, can be understood as the result of a large number of Germans willingly following him (reactions of followers) because he was an inspired orator and visionary who captured the mood of the moment (leader characteristics) at a time of collective misery during the depression of the

BOX 8.1 ALEXANDER: A MAN OF THE PEOPLE

> There are things generally regarded as rather unimportant but which are appreciated by soldiers. The fact that he exercised with his men, that he made his appearance little different from an ordinary citizen's, that he had the energy of a soldier. These characteristics, whether they were natural or consciously cultivated, had made him, in the eyes of his men, as much an object of affection as of awe.
>
> *Curtius, 1st century AD Roman Historian, writing about Alexander the Great, of the 4th century BC.*
>
> Nothing much seems to have changed since Alexander's time. Admired leaders and managers today often have the common touch and refuse to flaunt their positions. Some companies insist that managers spend a week a year dealing directly with customers, so that they do not lose touch with the essence of the business.
>
> In contrast, some companies still segregate the foot soldiers from the commanders. One high street retailer has one canteen for senior staff and one for junior staff at their head office. The senior staff canteen is in the head office building and so a short stroll along a few corridors; the junior ranks canteen is in another building over a busy road and means braving all weathers to get lunch. I once visited an organization that had four separate canteens for different levels of staff. Other organizations offer the status trappings of large offices, thick carpets and the company Jaguar for those at the top and shared, cold, draughty offices and battered chairs for others.

1930s and the humiliating defeat of the First World War (the particular situation).

There are a number of theories of charismatic leadership. We have already seen that Meindl views charisma as a process of romanticization. Other theories are those by House, the self-concept theory of Shamir and the attribution theory of Conger and Kanungo. We will look at each of these three in turn.

HOUSE'S THEORY OF CHARISMATIC LEADERSHIP

House's (1977) theory is a good example of the interactionist approach and emphasizes that charisma is about a special type of relationship between leader and follower. Followers believe that the leader's ideas are correct, accept the leader unquestioningly, feel affection for the leader, get emotionally involved in the organization's mission, set themselves high goals and believe that they can contribute to the success of the mission.

As an interactionist theory, it considers leader traits, leader behaviour and the situations that encourage charisma. The *traits* include a strong need for power, high self-confidence and strong conviction in their own views. Without these traits a leader is less likely to want to persuade and influence others and, if it is attempted, the endeavour is less likely to be successful.

The *behaviours* that a leader exhibits include *impression management*. By this is meant that the leader acts in a way designed to create the impression among followers that he or she is competent. Examples of impression management include talking about past successes, displaying considerable confidence and brushing off setbacks as irrelevant or trivial. Other behaviours involve *setting an example*. This is more than just allowing followers to copy or model their behaviour on that of the leader. It helps followers identify with the leader's beliefs and values, and means the leader can exert considerable influence on the behaviour, motivation and satisfaction of followers. Leadership by example may include working long hours or having an empowering, consultative style in formal organizations. Or stealing, vandalizing or acting in an intimidating fashion in an informal group, such as a gang. Other important behaviours cited by the theory are *setting high expectations* about followers' performance while at the same time expressing confidence that the subordinate can achieve the task; providing an attractive *vision* of the future which relates to the values and hopes of followers; and *arousing motivation* relevant to the vision by appealing to followers' aspirations through rousing speeches or regular contact that stresses the emotional appeal of the vision. Such motives may include a need for achievement or affiliation, a need to achieve an excellent performance in work, or the need to defeat an enemy or competitor.

Conditions

Conditions have to be right for charismatic leadership to flourish. Charismatic leaders rely on appealing to the 'ideological goals' of followers. They relate the vision or mission to subordinates' deeply rooted values, ideals and aspirations. House thinks that charisma is most likely to arise in stressful situations. When there are stresses or crises, those with the traits and behaviours outlined above are more likely to be seen as charismatic. So charismatic leadership is more likely to be seen in a political leader in war-time, or peace-time crises, than in an industrial manager. It is more probable, too, in some industries or occupations than others. The crisis at Chrysler in the early 1980s brought in Lee Iacocca, who was seen in the 1980s as a charismatic leader who turned Chrysler around. By the early 1990s, though, with Chrysler losing $1 billion a year, the image was somewhat tarnished.

The nature of the work also encourages charisma. A video made to illustrate the book *In Search of Excellence* by Peters and Waterman (1982) shows a computer 'whiz kid' explaining what motivates him in his design of the early Apple Macintosh computer. He says:

> I'm certainly not doing it for the sake of Steve Jobs [the founder of Apple]. I'm doing it for a much greater ideal than that. I'm doing it to change the way we see computers.

But in the same video, Steve Jobs is described by other computer experts in charismatic terms. It certainly seems that Jobs provided the conditions under which charisma, and creativity, could flourish. He set the design group apart, gave them enormous responsibility at a young age and as much freedom as they wanted. The result was a computer that truly did change our concept of personal computing, with its 'cute' image and intuitive software.

Appealing to the ideological goals of workers is particularly difficult when the task is repetitive or has little meaning or significance for them. Even here, though, it is possible. There's the regularly quoted story of two bricklayers in the Middle Ages. When asked what they are doing, one says: 'Building a wall, of course.' The other replies: 'Building a cathedral to the greater glory of God.'

Evidence

There are only a few studies that have tested House's theory, although these have been generally supportive.

At the conceptual level, there have been criticisms of House's theory on the basis that it defines charismatic leadership in terms of its effects or outcomes, rather than how it is perceived. The problem is that leaders who are not charismatic might have the same effect. In addition, it is theoretically suspect to define a concept solely in terms of its outcomes (Willner, 1984).

The empirical evidence is in favour of the theory, though. A study by Podsakoff *et al.* (1990) asked followers to describe their manager using a questionnaire. Managers who articulated a vision, modelled desirable behaviours and had high performance expectations of subordinates (all three behaviours characteristic of charismatic leaders) had subordinates who trusted their manager more, were more loyal and were more motivated to do extra work or to take more responsibility.

Work by Howell and Higgins (1990) involved content-analysing interviews with executives in 28 Canadian organizations. Some executives were seen as 'product champions', meaning that they had led the introduction of innovations in the organization, such as new products or methods. These product champions showed greater evidence of three of House's charismatic behaviours than did executives who were not product champions. These behaviours were communicating ideological goals, and showing both self-confidence and confidence in followers.

An intriguing study was conducted by House and colleagues on charismatic leadership in former presidents of the USA (House *et al.*, 1991). They set out to test the hypotheses from House's theory that charismatic American presidents would have high need for power, that charismatic behaviour would be related to presidential perform-ance and that charismatic behaviour would be more common among recent presidents compared with presidents from the more distant past. The assumption of greater frequency of charismatic presidents in recent years was based on the hypothesis that charisma is associated with crises and that there are more frequent political crises nowadays, plus the fact that the role of the president has changed to accentuate the visionary or ideological aspects of the role rather than the administrative one. The decision as to who was a charismatic president, and who not, was made by a panel of historians. They categorized 31 former presidents who had lasted at least two years of their first term of office. House *et al.* then content-analysed the presidents' inaugural speeches for power themes and images. To assess the presidents' charismatic behaviour, they consulted biographies of cabinet members to discover if presidents showed high levels of self-confidence, confidence in subordinates, high expectations of subordinates and strong ideological commitment. Leadership effectiveness was measured by ratings of prestige and greatness by a panel of historians and by analysis of their economic and social actions.

The study provided good support for House's theory. Need for power strongly predicted the level of charisma of presidents. Charismatic behaviours were positively related to ratings of performance, as were the frequency of crises. Charismatic leadership was more often associated with recent presidents rather than those in the more distant past.

In summary, it seems that charismatic people are needed when there are crises. One could argue that they are required more and more as time goes on, with the rapid pace of change and the challenges and threats in organizational life. Charisma is associated with the traits of need for power, and the outcomes of higher effectiveness ratings. Above all, the evidence is that charisma is called forth by a combination of traits, leader behaviours and the situation in which leaders find themselves.

THE ATTRIBUTION THEORY OF CONGER AND KANUNGO

The influential theory of Conger and Kanungo (1987) states that charisma is an attributional phenomenon. In other words, individuals in organizations attribute charisma to certain leaders under certain circumstances (see Chapter 4 for a discussion of attribution). The theory is also exclusively concerned with business leadership, not political leadership. A major concern of the theory is the types of behaviour on the part of leaders that make it likely that they will be seen as charismatic. Conger and Kanungo do not view charisma as some mystical or extraordinary quality possessed by just a few exceptional people, as Weber did. They imply that there is a set of ordinary behaviours which can be learned or adopted by a wide range of people. These *behaviours* are as follows.

Charisma is more likely to be attributed to leaders who describe a *vision* that paints a picture that is very different from the existing state of affairs. The vision must not be so different that followers view it as bizarre or unattainable, and nor should it be so similar to the *status quo* that it is not seen as a radical departure. Non-charismatic leaders opt for small incremental changes, or what Kirton (1984) describes as adaption (doing things better) rather than innovation (doing things differently). The vision defines the purpose of the change in a way that gives meaning to the tasks demanded of followers, a process Conger (1991) describes as 'framing'. They use *personal power*, perhaps based on their acknowledged expertise, to persuade and influence followers, rather than position power (see Chapter 6). *Persuasive appeals* through the use of emotive phrases which capture the imagination of followers are useful to convey the vision and motivate others towards its accomplishment.

Leaders who are *unconventional* in their methods of attaining the vision are more likely to be seen as charismatic. Unconventional methods that succeed encourage followers to ascribe exceptional expertise and skill to the leader. When leaders take *risks*, especially personal risks that threaten their reputation, money, or position in the organization, it increases the chance of them being seen as charismatic. Making sacrifices and incurring high costs is also part of risk taking. Box 8.2 outlines one leader's view of risk.

Concern for others, rather than concern for self, is associated with charisma, since followers are more likely to trust leaders who are interested in them as followers.

Leaders who show *self-confidence* and are enthusiastic about the vision are more likely to be viewed as charismatic than leaders who appear nervous or unconvinced of the worth of the new ideas. There is a self-fulfilling prophecy in all this. Followers are more likely to have confidence in leaders who themselves appear confident of the strategy and methods to implement it. So followers work harder, which increases the chance of success of the strategy.

Conditions

As with House's theory, Conger and Kanungo also stress that the conditions must be right for charismatic leadership to flourish. Leaders need to be *sensitive* to both the needs and desires of subordinates, and to the environment of the organization, so that the vision is in tune with both. The timing of strategic interventions is important. An innovation that is too late or premature is unlikely to work. Crises are more likely to encourage the emergence of charisma, or situations where subordinates are thoroughly

BOX 8.2 BRANSON ON RISK

Richard Branson, founder of Virgin Airlines, Virgin Records and a lot of smaller ventures, knows a lot about risk. He sets out a number of principles for managing the risk. These are:

- *Know the business*
Don't invest money in a business you don't know.

- *Be prepared to walk away from a deal*
Don't become so entranced by a business that you feel forced to invest. Remember that there is always another deal.

- *Limit the downside*
Do this by arranging the finance so that any borrowing or liabilities do not threaten the rest of the Group if they go wrong. Go for joint ventures which limit the downside risk. Have a way out of a high risk venture. Resist the temptation to invest more and more in a shaky enterprise.

- *Keep it small and cheap*
Branson keeps overheads small by running small offices in unfashionable areas, employing small numbers of people in lots of small organizations.

- *Commit yourself heart and soul*
This is the most important principle. As Branson says:

There is one overriding point I would like to make. Having done the evaluation of an investment and having applied all the rules I have listed and any others that you find particularly helpful in your markets, and having decided to make an investment, *do not pussyfoot around. Go for it!* In reality, one of the biggest risks that a lot of British industry takes is the lack of commitment to new projects and new ventures. They do not put enough energy, personal commitment and leadership into them.

Source: Branson, 'Risk taking', *Journal of General Management*, 1985, The Braybrooke Press Ltd, Henley-on-Thames, Oxon, UK.

disenchanted with the present state of affairs. A genuine crisis is not always necessary, though. The leader may be able to manufacture a crisis, or point out that the *status quo* is totally unacceptable, and then paint a picture of a more desirable future that followers can aspire to.

Evidence

Conger and Kanungo have provided a useful account of the process of charismatic leadership in organizations. The research base, though, is rather sparse at the present time. A major study is by Conger (1989) himself. He examined eight senior US business leaders. A panel of experts agreed that all eight were effective. Four of them were considered as charismatic and four not. He also used case studies based on leaders that are widely regarded as charismatic, such as Lee Iacocca of Chrysler, Donald Burr of the People Express airline, and Steve Jobs of Apple Computers. Data were collected by interviews with the executives and subordinates, direct observations of behaviour and company documents. Results showed that the behaviours and processes outlined in the model were associated with the attributions of charisma, as hypothesized.

A study by Puffer (1990) gave descriptions of a fictitious company and its general manager to undergraduates and managers. Descriptions were varied to test the effects of such factors as the manager's decision-making style and outcomes on the attributions of charisma. The study supported the attribution theory of Conger and Kanungo. An intuitive decision style and successful outcomes for the organization were associated with attributions of charisma. In addition, Puffer's work suggests that a manager's success in achieving outcomes encourages attributions of charisma, a factor that is underplayed in the Conger and Kanungo model.

Finally, the study by Howell and Higgins (1990) mentioned above also lends support to Conger and Kanungo's theory. Executives who were product champions used more charismatic behaviours than did executives who were not seen as product champions.

THE SELF-CONCEPT THEORY OF SHAMIR

The self-concept theory of Shamir and colleagues (Shamir, 1991; Shamir *et al.*, 1993) sets out to answer the question of why it is that charismatic leaders are able to influence subordinates fundamentally and motivate them to do extraordinary things. Why is it, for example, that they call forth extreme efforts or loyalty in employees? How is it that religious leaders can encourage followers to give up all worldly possessions? What inspires citizens to follow political leaders into war and possible death? According to Shamir and colleagues, recent motivation theory throws considerable light on these questions. The self-concept theory of charisma is similar to that of House but extends House's theory in the area of the motivational processes of charisma. These motivational and influence processes help explain the effects of leader behaviour on follower actions. There are four main concepts used by Shamir: personal identification, social identity, internalization and self-efficacy.

Personal identification means that the follower imitates the leader's behaviour or embraces the same attitudes so as to be like the leader. Gaining the leader's approval so as to satisfy followers' needs for acceptance and self-esteem may be part of the motivation for identification. Similarly, the follower gains higher self-esteem from the 'reflected glory' of associating with the leader if other people look up to the follower as a result of the association. So the influence the leader can exert from personal identification can be quite powerful. The power comes from the attractiveness of the leader for the subordinate; the more the attraction, the more the influence. Identification happens between leader and some subordinates but not others. Where the follower has low self-esteem, weak self-identity and a high need for dependence on authority figures, it is more likely to occur.

Personal identification is a process taking place in pairs, or 'dyads'. *Social identification*, on the other hand, is a collective process. It refers to identifying oneself with a collection of individuals such as a group, an organization or a nation. Being proud to be an employee of IBM, or feeling that membership of your local sports club is one of the most important aspects of your life, are examples of social identification. We will see in Chapter 12 that Hofstede describes cultures on a dimension of individualism–collectivism. Individuals, too, differ in terms of individualism–collectivism. High social identification is associated with a preference for a collectivist orientation. This means that the individual is prepared to put the needs of the group above his or her own and make personal sacrifices for the group. A charismatic leader can encourage social identification by trying to make the organization stand out from others, with a unique identity to which employees can associate themselves. A strong organization culture along with symbols such as logos, branding, emblems and common forms of dress, are some of the ways social identification can be strengthened. Rituals, such as singing the company song and group exercises before work, and ceremonies, such as sales jamborees and initiation rituals, are some of the others ways. Shamir views charismatic leadership as primarily a collective process in which social identification plays an important part in influencing followers.

Internalization, too, plays an important role in influencing others. This refers to the process by which subordinates internalize or 'take on board' the values and ideologies of the leader. They make the leader's vision their own. According to Shamir, one way the charismatic leader does this is to under-emphasize extrinsic rewards (such as pay or holiday entitlement) and stress intrinsic rewards, such as the satisfaction to be gained from the work itself, self-fulfilment or self-expression. Leaders stress that the future will be a better place as a result of their efforts. In its most extreme form, internalization leads to someone having difficulty separating work from the other aspects of their life. They *become* or *are* what they do. This is not as uncommon as it sounds. Professionals such as academics, doctors, TV and sports personalities, may internalize what they do for a living so that it becomes their life. Their work is inseparable from their self-concept. Bennis and Nanus (1985) quote the tightrope walker, Karl Wallenda. To him, walking the wire was living. Everything else was just waiting. Charismatic leaders sometimes manage to induce the same sentiments in followers.

Shamir's theory refers to both individual and collective *self-efficacy*. Individual self-efficacy is the belief that one is competent and capable of achieving one's task objectives. Collective self-efficacy is the belief that the group as a whole is competent and capable of achieving its goal: the belief that 'if we stand together, we will win'. If collective self-efficacy is high, group members will exert much greater effort for the common good. Charismatic leaders attempt to increase both individual and collective self-efficacy, so as to encourage followers to believe that exceptional feats can be achieved. Using the Wallenda example again, Bennis and Nanus note that he never ever thought of failure, which in his case meant certain death in a fall from the high wire. Only much later in his career did he start to think it was possible to fall; and fall he did. His widow noted that he had only recently given the risk any thought. Self-belief or self-efficacy certainly seems important to success.

Conditions

Shamir and his colleagues emphasize the reciprocal nature of charismatic leadership. Charismatic leaders are more likely to emerge when they need to espouse a vision that is compatible with followers' values and ideology, and followers actively seek leaders who share their values. The most adept charismatic leaders are able to tune into the needs and values of followers. They can sometimes articulate values and ideas that followers may not have put into words.

It is easier for charismatic leaders to emerge in organizations where followers have a strong set of values, such as health-care or education, rather than in the manufacture of arms or tobacco, for example. Shamir, like House, feels that charismatic leadership is more likely where there is unstructured work, as opposed to routine, repetitive work and where employees are more interested in extrinsic rewards such as pay. But he places less stress on crisis situations as a precursor for charismatic leadership. He does note, though, that organizations that are floundering, where employees are worried and where future success is unlikely, are fertile breeding grounds for charisma.

Evidence

Shamir and colleagues' theory is too recent to have been subjected to empirical test. However, there is good evidence from such motivational theories as expectancy theory, and from self-concept theory, to lead us to believe that their theory is an interesting development and worth further research.

SUMMARY

Charisma is not simply a gift or personal trait possessed by some individuals, but more a special type of relationship which exists between leaders and followers. Conditions have to be right for charismatic leadership to develop and flourish. All the available research suggests that the right conditions need to include a combination of traits, leader behaviours, situation and a vision which is shared by the leader and followers. This concept of a 'shared vision' has similarities to the notion of transformational leadership, which we discuss next, although some researchers believe that there are major differences between the two types of leadership.

9 *Transformational leadership*

The terms 'charismatic leadership', used in the previous chapter, and 'transformational leadership', described here, are sometimes used interchangeably by writers. I have chosen to treat them separately in this book, since, although there are overlaps in how they describe leadership, the two terms do not mean the same thing.

Transformational leadership should also be distinguished from *transactional leadership*. Much of the early part of the book was concerned with transactional approaches, and it was not until the work of Burns and Bass that the term 'transforming' (Burns, 1978) or 'transformational' (Bass, 1985) started to be used. For Burns, transactional leadership is a process of motivating followers by appealing to their self-interest and exchanging, say, pay and status for effort. Transforming leadership is a process in which leaders and followers raise each other to higher levels of morality and motivation.

Bass (1985) defined the transactional leader as one who:

1   recognizes what his or her followers want to get from their work and tries to see that followers get what they desire if their performance warrants it;
2   exchanges rewards and promises of rewards for appropriate levels of effort;
3   responds to the self-interests of followers as long as they are getting the job done.

So transactional leadership behaviours are those behaviours which concerned the early theorists. Transactional leaders clarify the role of subordinates, show consideration towards them, initiate structure, reward and punish, and attempt to meet the social needs of subordinates.

Transformational leadership is more concerned with 'engagement' between leaders and followers. Leaders attempt to engage the full person of the subordinate and enthuse them. They arouse in their subordinates a heightened awareness of the key issues for the group or the organization. They seek to concern subordinates with achievement, growth and development.

Bernard Bass is the researcher who has done most to describe and investigate transformational leadership. He has developed a questionnaire called the Multifactor Leadership Questionnaire (MLQ) based on his model of transactional and transformational leadership. The MLQ enables subordinates to describe their leader on seven dimensions: four transformational ones, two transactional ones and *laissez-faire*, described by Bass as non-transacting and the absence of true leadership. (Earlier work had three transformational behaviours, but Bass and Avolio, 1990, later added a fourth.) The seven dimensions are as follows:

1 *Laissez-faire.*
2 Management-by-exception.
3 Contingent reward.
4 Individualized consideration.
5 Intellectual stimulation.
6 Inspirational motivation.
7 Idealized influence.

NON-TRANSACTING

Laissez-faire, or 'where's the leadership?'. This describes a leader who is not actively involved in followers' work. The leader avoids taking a stand on issues, refrains from intervening, lets others do as they please and is absent, disorganized and indifferent. Follower reactions include conflict with each other about their responsibilities and attempts to usurp the leader's role. The US president, Calvin Coolidge, for example, is reputed to have slept 11 hours a day and adopted a policy of remaining aloof from as much of the day-to-day affairs as he could. Similarly, Indira Gandhi, the prime minister of India from 1966 until her assassination in 1984, has been accused of being too *laissez-faire* and lacking the ability to react to avoid food crises and political instability. A critic, Jayapra-kash Narayan, said: 'My impression has been that one of her favourite methods of dealing with issues has been to put them on the shelf and let them be forgotten for a while and let events find their own solution.'

TRANSACTIONAL LEADERSHIP

1 *Management-by-exception*, or leadership by correcting mistakes. This is when a leader applies correct action, such as reprimands, when, and only when, an employee commits an error or fails to deliver on agreed objectives. The leader does not attempt to change methods of work if subordinates are achieving performance goals. Leaders take no action unless a problem arises.

There are two forms of management-by-exception (MBE), passive MBE and active MBE. With *passive MBE*, the leader sets standards but waits for deviations to occur. When they do, the leader corrects, but tends to intervene reluctantly. *Active MBE* describes the leader who sets standards but monitors for deviations to occur, then corrects. He or she searches for errors and is alert to mistakes. Followers with either active or passive MBE leaders tend to avoid initiating change and risk taking, preferring instead to maintain the *status quo*. Hardly a desired state of affairs in most present-day organizations.

2 *Contingent reward*, or leadership by exchanging promises for results. This is the familiar work-for-reward exchange agreement, where the leader makes clear what tasks must be accomplished in order to obtain desired rewards and provides these rewards only when subordinates perform adequately or put in the necessary effort. The leader provides support in exchange for required effort and gives praise where deserved. Mary Kay Ash, founder and owner of Mary Kay cosmetics in the US, is often referred to as a transformational leader (see Box 9.1). Yet she does not ignore contingent reward. She praises her salespeople (called consultants) in public and rewards the top performers with pink Cadillacs, a 'trophy on wheels'. This signals to everyone the value placed by the organization on outstanding performance and the rewards that can be obtained.

BOX 9.1 MARY KAY COSMETICS

Most women in Britain have heard of Avon cosmetics, the direct selling organization, where salespeople sell directly and independently to customers. Mary Kay Cosmetics, founded by Mary Kay Ash while a single mother in her forties, is the major competitor to Avon in the US. When Mary Kay was a saleswoman with another company, she was rewarded for one outstanding achievement with a light used in fishing. She vowed then that, if ever she had her own business, she would never reward her people with such ill-conceived prizes.

The philosophy of the company is to reward employees on the basis of what they achieve. Second, remembering the fish light episode, the company rewards with things the employees value. Third, the company is 'female friendly'. The female sales force can work hours that suit their domestic responsibilities. Mary Kay Ash wanted women to have rewards based on performance, not on the basis of sex, with the right and opportunity to earn the same as men. And reward them it does! It has been reported that Mary Kay Cosmetics have more women earning over $50,000 than any other US company. The company also claims that more black women earn these figures than in any other company in the world. Other rewards include pink Cadillacs, holidays, jewellery and expensive clothes, all distributed to top sales women in carefully staged 'Pageant Nights'.

There is more to the success of Mary Kay Cosmetics than performance-related pay though. Mary Kay Ash is often cited as a charismatic leader. She is a considerable orator (though she says it took her years to develop the skill), has a magnetic power over others, has a reputation for hard work and struggling with adversity (her single-parent status), and gives meaning to the lives of the distributors by appealing to higher ideals of women's independence, not just material rewards.

TRANSFORMATIONAL LEADERSHIP

Bass views transformational leadership and transactional leadership as processes that are distinct but not mutually exclusive. A leader may use both types of leadership at different times and in different situations.

In the Bass model, transformational leadership has four components known as the 'four I's'.

1 *Individualized consideration*, or leadership by developing people. This refers to the care that the leader shows towards subordinates about their development and about them as individuals. The leader is alert to followers' needs, provides challenges and learning opportunities and delegates to raise their skill and confidence. The result is that followers are more likely to be willing to develop competence and take initiative.

2 *Intellectual stimulation*, or leadership by stimulating people to think. Here the leader encourages followers to use their imagination and to challenge the accepted ways of doing things. The leader re-examines assumptions, creates a broad, imaginative picture, and is willing to accept apparently foolish ideas. The message is that followers should feel free to think and imagine. This type of leadership is essential when change and innovation are required.

The case of the Swiss watch industry is a useful analogy for the power of intellectual stimulation. In the 1960s, the Swiss watch was the epitome of watchmaking, with its finely crafted gears and superb accuracy. The Swiss dominated the watch industry and employed 65,000 people. By the early 1980s, that number had halved, and the market was dominated by the quartz watch manufactured in Hong Kong, Taiwan and South Korea. Quartz watches are so much cheaper to manufacture and give excellent accuracy. Yet the seeds of failure lay in the hands of the Swiss. The idea for the quartz watch came from Switzerland, but they thought little of the idea. Swiss manufacturers presented the idea to a meeting of the watch industry, and representatives from both Texas Instruments and Seiko were there. It was they who saw the potential and developed it.

As Levitt, the editor of *Harvard Business Review*, noted, 'nothing characterizes the successful organization so much as its willingness to abandon what has long been successful'. Some organizations strive for constant change, even when successful, as Box 9.2 describing Hewlett–Packard shows.

BOX 9.2 CHANGE WHILE YOU ARE AHEAD

Hewlett–Packard (HP) was a scientific instrument venture formed by Bill Hewlett and David Packard in the USA in 1939. Since then it has grown to be the second largest US computer company in terms of revenue, second in the world for computer workstations and the world market leader in 'open systems' (industry standards) minicomputers, computer printers and test and measurement equipment. The founding fathers' strength was that they were engineers who enjoy inventing products. The base remains today. HP is mostly run by engineers. This core strength means that HP is able to bring new technology to market fast, even if it means taking sales away from its existing products, something its competitors avoid.

You would think, then, that HP had everything going for it. Yet resting on its laurels is not something HP is keen to do. Some inside the company claim HP stands for 'healthy paranoia'. They are always looking over their shoulder at the competitors, and thinking about the next move. The chief executive, Lew Platt, is passionate about it. He realizes that it is too easy to keep doing what you are doing today for just a little bit too long.

> General Motors, Sears, IBM were the greatest companies in their industries, the best of the best in the world. These companies did not make gigantic mistakes. They were not led by stupid, inept people. The only real mistake they made was to keep doing whatever it was that had made them successful for a little too long. . . . The real secret is to build an organization that isn't afraid to make changes while it is still successful, before change becomes imperative for survival.*

This doesn't necessarily mean reorganization. HP prefers 'cross-organizational teams' rather than restructuring its operations. Such teams help the organization to react faster. This is particularly important in the fastest moving markets, such as video communications, where product development cycles

> have come down from two to five years, to six to nine months, in the last few years. In March 1994, Platt was quoted in the *Financial Times* as saying:
>
>> Whatever we're doing that made us successful today won't be good in 2 years' time. It might work this year. Maybe it'll even work next year, but it will kill you the year after that.
>
> *Note:* *Quoted in the *Financial Times*, 18 March 1994.

3 *Inspirational motivation*, or leadership by inspiring people. The leader creates a clear picture of the future state that is both optimistic and attainable, encourages others to raise their expectations, reduces complexity to key issues and uses simple language to convey the mission. The reaction of followers is increased willingness to exert extra effort so as to try to achieve the mission.

4 *Idealized influence*, or leadership by charisma. This means that the leader attempts to be a role model. He or she shows great persistence and determination in pursuing objectives, takes full responsibility for his or her actions and demonstrates supreme confidence in the vision. Leaders sacrifice self-gain for the gain of others and share the success and the limelight. Followers' reactions are an emotional attraction to the leader, a greater willingness to trust the leader and attempts to be similar.

All seven approaches to leadership can be enacted in a directive or participative way, as shown in Tables 9.1 and 9.2. The model argues that transformational leaders must also be transactional in certain situations to be effective. It is not a question of one or the other.

TRANSFORMATIONAL AND CHARISMATIC LEADERSHIP

The idealized influence aspect of transformational leadership is very close to the charismatic leader, discussed in the previous chapter. However, according to Bass, there are major differences between transformational and charismatic leaders.

Table 9.1 Directive versus participative nontransactional and transactional leadership

A *laissez-faire* leader can be:

Directive	*or*	*Participative*
'If my followers need answers to questions, let them find the answers themselves.'		'Whatever you think is the correct choice is OK with me.'

A management-by-exception leader can be:

Directive	*or*	*Participative*
'There are rules and this is how you have violated them.'		'Let's develop the rules together that we will use to identify mistakes.'

A contingent-reward leader can be:

Directive	*or*	*Participative*
'If you achieve the objectives I've set, I will recognize your accomplishment with the following reward.'		'Let's agree on what has to be done and how you will be rewarded if you achieve the objectives.'

Source: Adapted from *Full Range Leadership Development*, Avolio and Bass (1991).

Charisma is a necessary but not sufficient component of transformational leadership. Some individuals, such as movie stars, are charismatic but have no transformational effects on the majority of followers. Followers may dress like the star, or imitate their behaviour, but are unlikely to be disinterested in themselves and follow a cause.

Transformational leaders influence followers by arousing strong emotions, but do so for benign reasons. They seek to empower followers by developing their independence and building their confidence. They seek the improvement of the individual, the organization or the society. Charismatic leaders, in contrast, sometimes seek to enslave followers by keeping them weak and dependent. They are interested in personal loyalty, rather than attachment to values and ideals. The contrast is between Martin Luther King or Mahatma Gandhi, who used their charismatic powers to improve the lot of their followers and society, and Michael Koresh, many of whose followers died in the fire of the Waco siege, or Jim Jones.

Table 9.2 Directive versus participative transformational leadership

An individually considerate leader can be:

Directive	*or*	*Participative*
'I will provide the support you need in your efforts to develop yourself in the job.'		'What can we do as a group to give each other the necessary support to develop our capabilities?'

An intellectually stimulating leader can be:

Directive	*or*	*Participative*
'You must re-examine the assumption that a cold fusion engine is a physical impossibility. Revisit this problem and question your assumption.'		'Can we try to look at our assumptions as a group without being critical of each other's ideas until all assumptions have been listed?'

An inspirationally motivating leader can be:

Directive	*or*	*Participative*
'You need to say to yourself every day you are getting better. You must look at your progression and continue to build upon it over time.'		'Let's work together to merge our aspirations and goals for the good of our group.'.

A leader showing idealized influence can be:

Directive	*or*	*Participative*
'I've made the decision so there's no going back. You must trust me and my direction to achieve what we have set out to do.'		'We can be a winning team because of our faith in each other. I need your support to achieve our mission.'

Source: Adapted from *Full Range Leadership Development*, Avolio and Bass (1991).

Jones was a cult leader who convinced his followers to move from the USA to Guyana for a better spiritual life. One year later, over 900 of his congregation were encouraged by Jim Jones to commit suicide.

Jones was interested in self-aggrandizement, not the improvement of the lot of others. Transformational leaders are interested in followers thinking for themselves, and thinking creatively. Jim Jones inspired others to follow the vision as he felt society should be. Transformational leaders inspire others to develop themselves, develop the team, and develop the vision further.

Although Bass treats charisma and transformational leadership as distinct concepts, many writers do not. The work of Tichy and Devanna (1986) on transformational leadership, for example, talks about articulating a vision which enthuses followers and creates considerable loyalty and trust. This sounds very similar to charisma. So while conceptually they may be distinct, much of the writing fails to make it clear that they are.

Trice and Beyer (1991) make the distinction between charisma and transformational leadership by suggesting that charismatic leaders often create new organizations, while transformational leaders change existing organizations. This fits well with anecdotal evidence, with Richard Branson of Virgin, Mary Kay Ash of Mary Kay Cosmetics and Anita Roddick of The Body Shop, all described as charismatic founders of their companies. However, since charisma, like beauty, lies in the eye of the beholder, who is to say that individuals such as Lee Iacocca, who rescued Chrysler, or John Harvey-Jones, who steered ICI, should not be called charismatic? They are undoubtedly seen as such by some.

Evidence

Bass's work on transformational leadership has stimulated a large number of studies. In particular, the MLQ has been a useful tool to investigate the relationship of transformational leadership to other variables, such as follower satisfaction or leader effectiveness. This research is very usefully reviewed by Bryman (1992), who points out that:

1   Idealized influence (charismatic leadership) and inspirational leadership tend to be the components of Bass's theory that are most likely to be associated with favourable outcomes, such as effectiveness, satisfaction and extra effort.
2   Individualized consideration and intellectual stimulation are usually the next most important components. Individualized consideration is typically more important than intellectual stimulation, except when extra effort is the outcome measure.
3   Contingent reward makes a fairly important contribution to satisfaction, effectiveness and extra effort.

4 Management-by-exception produces inconsistent results. Passive management-by-exception seems to be less effective than its active form.

5 *Laissez-faire* leadership is highly undesirable.

Bryman concludes that 'Bass's framework for examining transformational and transactional leadership has produced an impressive array of findings which possess a good deal in common' (1992: 128). However, he also notes that the MLQ questionnaire method used in the studies has the same problems as we noted in Chapter 2 with the Ohio State studies, which used a similar questionnaire, the Leader Behavior Description Questionnaire (LBDQ).

The *correlational design* of most of the MLQ studies gives particular problems. Because two factors are correlated does not imply that one causes the other. So it is not possible to separate out whether effectiveness causes attributions of transformational leadership, or whether transformational leadership causes greater effectiveness. All we know is that the two are linked.

One possible reason why they are linked is the *common method variance* problem. Many of the studies have taken measures of perceptions of leader behaviour and measures of perceived effectiveness at the same time and from the same followers. So correlations between behaviour and performance could be artificially increased by the tendency for respondents to answer questions consistently. Where studies have used independent measures of effectiveness, the findings are similar to those in which subordinates provide both leader perceptions and performance measures, but the correlations are quite a lot smaller. A study by Yammarino and Bass (1990), for example, found that there was a correlation of 0.87 when subordinates provided measures of both transformational leadership and performance (the common method variance problem) but only 0.34 when there were independent measures of performance.

Despite the problems, though, the MLQ is a major step forward in the investigation of transformational leadership, and the studies generally show that transformational leaders are rated as significantly more effective than transactional leaders.

OTHER WORK ON TRANSFORMATIONAL LEADERSHIP

The strength of Bass's work is that it is mostly questionnaire based. This means that hypotheses can be tested, the results challenged or replicated, and there are quantitative results which give greater precision to the findings. Two other studies of transformational leaders are descriptive, being based on interviews with leaders, and so do not share these strengths. However, the results do have a rich, vivid feel about them, and provide many insights into the essence of transformational leadership and what leaders do.

RESEARCH ON TWELVE CHIEF EXECUTIVES, BY TICHY AND DEVANNA

Tichy and Devanna (1986) studied twelve chief executives in mostly large organizations. They interviewed the executives themselves and occasionally others in the organization. Analysis of the interviews led Tichy and Devanna to describe the transformational leadership process as a series of three phases:

- recognizing the need for change;
- creating a new vision;
- institutionalizing the changes.

The first step for the leader is to *recognize the need to revitalize the organization*. Gradual changes in the external and internal environment of the organization may easily go unrecognized until it is too late. Handy (1994) talks about the live frog in a saucepan of water slowly heated up over a flame. Sudden changes would make the frog jump out. Slow changes are not perceived, the frog stays where it is, and the inevitable happens – dead frog. For dead frog read the British motor cycle industry in the 1960s or the Swiss watch industry in the 1970s. A key role for a leader is to alert others to the incremental changes and to take the threat seriously. As noted in the Hewlett–Packard example (see Box 9.2), this is especially difficult when the organization is thriving. It is vital, none the less. Tichy and Devanna claim that any organization that fails to revitalize and transform itself risks failure. They list four ways a leader can alert followers to the environmental changes and the threats they pose:

- Challenge assumptions by playing devil's advocate and encouraging opposing views.
- Develop external networks. Encourage outsiders to critique the organization. Persuade insiders to get involved in other employees' jobs (e.g. engineers going on the road with salespeople) to bring a new perspective on the familiar.
- Encourage employees from all functions to visit other organizations, including those overseas, to see how they do things.
- Benchmark (measure performance against those of competitors). Measure not just financial matters, such as earnings or market share, but quality, customer satisfaction, labour turnover, and so on. Distribute the information widely in the organization to reduce complacency.

After people have been alerted to the fact that change is necessary, the leader's next step is to manage the transition. This involves deciding specifically what changes are necessary and handling the resistance to the change. Changes are likely to mean alterations in the power and status of some individuals, frustrated career expectations, and the learning of new skills and ways of doing things. The role of the leader is to smooth the path by building employees' self-confidence, facilitating the learning of new methods and convincing people that they are not personally responsible for the previous failures.

Creating a new vision is something that almost all writers on transformational leadership emphasise. The vision points the way to a new state of affairs. It is an appealing picture of a more desirable future. It inspires people to believe that the future is worth the upheaval of undoing the present. A vision needs to be a source of self-esteem and a common purpose for members of the organization.

According to Tichy and Devanna's research, visions are rarely the product of one individual. They are formed by a collective process of participation and consultation, evolved over a period of time. Participation not only makes it more likely that an appropriate vision for the organization will emerge, it also increases the likelihood that the vision will be accepted and internalized by those who have to make it happen.

Institutionalizing the changes refers to the fact that all of the above cannot be accomplished by one person or even a handful of individuals. The leader needs the active support and help of all the key players in the organization. This may mean some changes in personnel since the chief executive's team must be fully committed to the vision. Whether new personnel or existing ones, however, the leader needs a network of relationships with influential members of the organization. If they have participated in creating the vision, it again means that these significant employees will be more committed to making the changes happen throughout the organization.

Evidence

Interesting as it is, this research cannot be considered good research. For one thing, there is no comparison group of non-transformational leaders, or failed leaders. So it is dangerous to assume that only successful transformational leaders follow the steps outlined above. Maybe other leaders do too. Maybe other factors are associated with organizational success, not the three steps that these twelve leaders identify as characteristic behaviours. Without comparison groups, there is no way of knowing. It is also risky to generalize from just twelve carefully selected individuals.

In addition, Tichy and Devanna updated the study in the second edition of their book four years later. In it they note that some of the companies are struggling. In particular, the two computer companies had failed to cope with the rapidly changing competitive environment for their products. So what faith can we place in the authors' view that their transformational leaders were able to respond to environmental pressure and transform the organization appropriately?

Nevertheless, the research makes entertaining reading and provides a fund of ideas which can be tested by more rigorous means.

RESEARCH ON 90 LEADERS BY BENNIS AND NANUS

Bennis and Nanus (1985) interviewed 90 prominent and successful leaders in the USA, of whom 60 were chief executives in the private sector, while the other 30 included people from the public sector, politicians, conductors of symphony orchestras and the founder of a ballet school. All the leaders had created new ideas, new policies and new ways of doing things. Interviews lasted three to four hours and ten of the leaders were observed for around five days.

The research suggests that effective leaders develop four strategies which together define the essence of leadership. First there is *management of attention through vision.* Leadership requires the capacity to imagine a desired state of affairs, to develop the kind of image of the future that induces enthusiasm and commitment in others. Management of attention through vision is the creating of focus. A vision must inspire others, transforming purpose into action. When the vision is shared by others in the organization they have a sense of direction and can place their own position in relation to where the organization is going. Members become empowered because they feel motivated and directed by the enticing vision of the future which the leader describes. Bennis and Nanus cite the example of Sergiu Comisslana, conductor of the Houston Symphony Orchestra, who knew exactly what he wanted to hear from the orchestra. A member of the orchestra referred to it as 'the maestro's tapestry of intentions'.

The second step is to create *meaning through communication.* Strategies one and two are mutually exclusive; it is no good having vision if you cannot communicate its meaning to others. Comisslana's obsessive regard for the outcome, knowing exactly what he wanted, would have been useless without his ability to convey it to the orchestra. Leaders have to persuade others of the rightness of their vision and communicate it, not just inside the organization but it must be recognized by suppliers, consumers and others outside the organization too. Leaders must constantly restate the vision and its desirability. It will also usually be necessary to change the organization structure in line with the vision and the values it embodies. A few years ago I was commissioned to help an organization move from being a traditional accountancy firm to a more market-led and entrepreneurial financial services organization (Shackleton, 1992). The new managing partner's vision of where the firm should be in five years' time would have been impossible to implement without constant reiteration, partners' acceptance of the changes, training of the partners and structural changes in line with the vision and values.

The leader must also *manage trust through constancy.* Without mutual trust the leader blazing the new path will be viewed with suspicion and so be unable to empower others. In addition, the leader must be predictable and consistent, such that his or her actions are compatible with the vision and values.

Finally, there is *management of self* which includes *positive self-regard* and *positive other regard.* Leaders have to have considerable belief in themselves to overcome the opposition that change so often brings and to continue to have faith in their vision. Positive other regard involves a parallel belief in those around the leader that they can be empowered to carry the vision forward. According to Bennis and Nanus, this factor was 'perhaps the most impressive and memorable quality of the leaders we studied'. They use the example of Polaroid as illustration. Edwin Land, the founder of Polaroid, continually motivated his team to 'achieve the impossible' of the instant camera. His absolute conviction in himself convinced his managers that they too could not fail. This refusal to contemplate failure is a key element of management or deployment of self through positive self-regard.

Evidence

While this research is entertaining and informative, it does suffer from the same problems as the work of Tichy and Devanna. The main one is that there is no comparison group of managers to compare with the 90 leaders, or even 90 unsuccessful leaders. So how do we know that these strategies are exclusive to successful leaders? Maybe managers or transactional leaders employ these strategies too. So we risk glorifying visionary leaders at the expense of managers.

A second problem is that the results come directly from conversations with the leaders themselves. We have no external check that this is really how they behave. For example, the positive self-regard strategy was elicited by the question 'what are your major strengths and weaknesses?'. Bennis and Nanus report that the leaders emphasized their strengths. Such results lead one to believe that different results might have been obtained if subordinates or members of the team had been questioned. Yet the view that having and communicating a vision, building trust and being consistent are important, is supported by other research.

Once again, though, Bennis and Nanus's book makes entertaining and stimulating reading. It has been widely quoted and the ideas are often used on leadership development courses. It has an intuitive appeal to practising managers. Nor are the results that dissimilar from those found with better designed studies, such as those using the MLQ. But until it has been substantiated by more robust methods, the research results have to be treated cautiously.

SUMMARY

We have seen in this chapter that most researchers agree that transformational leadership involves creating a new vision which points the way to a new state of affairs for a more desirable future. The vision becomes a catalyst for inspiring others towards a common purpose for the group to achieve and also helps to create self-esteem in members of the group. As Tichy and Devanna have observed, visions are rarely the product of one individual alone but are formed by a collective process of participation and consultation. This process makes the members more committed to the proposed changes and more motivated and directed towards the vision. The collective process also creates a feeling of empowerment within members of the group as they work together towards the vision created by the leader.

10 *Empowerment*

WHAT IS EMPOWERMENT?

Empowerment is a philosophy of giving more responsibility and decision-making authority to more junior people in the organization. This may involve quite small shifts in the patterns of power and authority. In most organizations, the aspects of their job over which employees are intended to be empowered may be clearly defined, and are certainly likely to be restricted. The more clearly the areas are defined, the more likely it is that the workforce will become empowered.

Although superficially the same, empowerment is very different from delegation. In delegation, one individual – the leader, manager or supervisor – decides to pass on a task or a specific part of his or her job to another individual for a specific reason. These reasons vary, but include subordinate development, or freeing up one's own time, or because the task is low risk. This may be a one-off action, or it may be for a longer period, but it is a 'contract' or exchange between two people or between a leader and his or her team. Empowerment, on the other hand, is a philosophy of management. It widens the responsibility associated with the current task or role without necessarily changing the task or role itself. It is intended to operate across a very broad front, perhaps a whole company, a division or a particular function. Whatever the scope, the boundaries of empowerment may be broad or very narrow, depending on the intentions of the changes.

For example, in a machine shop, machinists were empowered to change the tool or the tip whenever they judged for themselves that the existing tip was sufficiently worn to affect the quality of the output. However, the order in which pieces were machined was still determined by the 'planner'. In the past, the tips were replaced based on a formula involving machining time and materials machined, not as a result of the machinist's decision. This was undoubtedly empowerment, but with a relatively restricted boundary.

ORIGINS OF EMPOWERMENT

There is no one single cause or origin of the empowerment movement. Rather, it emerges from the increasing specialization of some work, the changing shape of organizations and a shift towards placing greater value on the human being at work.

Specialization of work

Some sectors of industry and commerce have become increasingly dependent on expert workers, sometimes called knowledge workers or talented workers (Sadler, 1993), who are bright, educated and motivated, and often difficult to manage. Financial services, research and development (R&D) and education are just some of the examples. Devising approaches which reduce the amount of time and effort which goes into managing such people has several benefits. Most expert workers are much happier to work with minimal supervision, and are more likely to remain with their employer, as long as they are afforded the opportunity to keep up to date. Empowerment suits both managers and subordinates.

The changing shape of organizations

As organizations have delayered (the removal of a tier of manage-ment) to produced leaner, flatter structures, managers have found themselves with larger numbers reporting to them, and bigger gaps between them and their subordinates, in hierarchical terms and in terms of functions. In a similar way to the 'expert worker', this delayering potentially increases the difficulty of managing across a large span, particularly where this involves managers in supervising work outside their areas of expertise. Thus again the need to relinquish some of the responsibility to those who are better equipped to decide.

Valuing the individual

Leaders frequently make statements along the lines 'people are our most important asset'. Some early writing on empowerment (e.g. Block, 1987) used this starting point, arguing that people behaved responsibly if treated as such. In fact, they often surpass the most optimistic expectations. Some of the early exponents did not, however, give much attention to the extent to which cultural change was necessary.

Quality circles, so much the 'current flavour' in the 1970s, provided a forum where employees at all levels could discuss the problems they encountered. These were largely confined to issues in their own work area. Many of the problems involved changes of a very minor nature; this led some managers to question why employees didn't feel able to take the corrective action on their own. In addition, few 'quality circles' proved to be self-sustaining. So giving employees more responsibility in these areas was in some instances a natural consequence of the demise of the earlier initiative.

AIMS OF EMPOWERMENT

Improved quality

Empowerment philosophy suggests that decisions should be made by people closest to the action, whether it is processing paper, working on a production line or providing a face-to-face service to customers. These are the people who are most familiar with normal or acceptable performance and therefore most able to detect variations or other problems. Where the overriding drive is for quality, the aim of empowerment is to catch the faulty work at the earliest stage possible. This saves the costs of reworking and also minimizes the chance of faulty products or services getting to the customer.

All-round benefits

The above obviously creates a risk that the customer will receive no goods or services rather than faulty ones. Empowerment within any organization usually has some checks which aim to minimize this non-delivery. These safeguards can in themselves derail the empowerment initiative by appearing to give responsibility with one hand and taking it away with the other. The aim of any successful move to increase empowerment incorporates clear benefits for employees, customers and the employing organization. Where any one of these is neglected, successful implementation is unlikely.

Reduced dependence on the rule book

In many organizations, particularly those where there is great concern about status and hierarchical position, an over-dependence on caution and following rules can stifle initiative and change and even lead to situations where common sense is left behind when employees arrive at work. Empowerment is then seen as a way of encouraging employees to bring the 'whole' of themselves to work, and increasing productivity, while simultaneously decreasing passive acceptance of embedded practices.

THE INTRODUCTION OF EMPOWERMENT

There is a real dilemma for any leader wanting to empower his or her workforce. An individual (or a top team) who decides to go down this route, and then plans the implementation, behaves hierarchically. Yet this is the antithesis of empowerment. The challenge is to find a way of starting down this road while simultaneously behaving in a way which is congruent with the plan. This is paramount whatever the circumstances or scope of the introduction.

In most organizations empowerment involves a change in culture. So the size and difficulty of the change should not be underestimated, nor the need for investment of time and energy (see Box 10.1). Theories of change (see Plant, 1987, for example) range from starting by fully understanding the present, to painting a clear picture of the future vision as the clear goal to strive for. Similarly with empowerment. Some exponents advocate a company-wide change, arguing that empowerment cannot thrive in a pocket. Others propose starting with a 'warm' area – a part of the company where there is already enthusiasm or a particularly urgent need to make change. The latter provides more scope for involving the workforce in an empowering way in starting to explore what will be involved, where the boundaries should lie, what benefits can be expected and for whom, what training is needed, what other information will need to be provided on a regular basis, what the likely barriers to success are and how they can be minimized. In this smaller-scale introduction, a leader who is able to practise an empowering style of leadership from

BOX 10.1   IGNITION SESSIONS AT MERCURY COMMUNICATIONS

Mike Harris is the chief executive of Mercury Communications, the British Telecom competitor. In 1993, he instituted a process of employee empowerment at Mercury, and chose an unusual and controversial technique to help him change the culture. Over a period of six months, the majority of Mercury's 11,000 staff attended 'ignition' sessions in huge canvas igloos located in a car park at Birmingham's National Exhibition Centre. At night the igloos were lit up, and were visible from the adjacent motorway. The intense training programme lasted up to ten hours and involved emotional debate, self-disclosure, and much applause, all interspersed with a sound and light show reminiscent of *Top of the Pops* music videos or American-style cults. The technique has been variously described as brainwashing and mindbending, or as a highly effective and enriching experience that trains and motivates employees towards an exciting future.

The aim of the process was to introduce staff to the culture of empowerment. Employee empowerment involves putting the employee first, not the customer. It claims to produce a more motivated, committed, thinking workforce, who take individual responsibility for the quality of the product or service, and customer satisfaction. Employees are encouraged to come up with suggestions for improving all parts of the organization, from small details of working methods to whole new product ideas, and are often financially rewarded for doing so. Mercury claims it had hundreds of workable ideas and that many new products were introduced in record time as a direct result of the 'ignition' sessions.

The concept of empowerment is not new. Nor is it unique to Mercury. Many companies in Britain have embraced the concept of empowerment, including Elida Gibbs (a Unilever company), Rank Xerox, British Airways and Rover. Few, though, have taken such an extreme approach to imbuing employees with an understanding of an empowerment culture.

Source: Adapted from 'Mindbenders explore the future at Mercury', *The Sunday Times*, 24 April 1994.

the outset is likely to provide a role model for others to follow. The qualities likely to have most impact include listening skills, an openness to new and different ideas, an ability to be encouraging and to avoid being judgemental. Patience is also needed, to give those who are unused to generating ideas, decision-making and problem-solving the time to build their confidence and learn new skills. If there are problems, it is very tempting for those used to taking a strong leadership role to step in and provide their own ideas or solutions.

BOX 10.2 EMPOWERMENT: REPACKAGED FAD?

To the cynic, empowerment is just another in a long line of management fads. Even those who make a living out of consulting to management, such as Richard Pascale the American consultant, talk about a 'fads industry'. He asks: 'Are we just repackaging or are we really coming up with new discoveries?'

True, empowerment looks a lot like some earlier fads, such as 'employee involvement' or 'job enrichment'. Many organizations 'involve' or 'empower' employees without labelling it as such. Yet whatever we wish to call it, the main aim of these fads is to motivate employees and allow them to feel a greater sense of involvement and commitment to their work.

If you walk into one of Forte's Harvester restaurants you can see staff teams doing their own recruitment, devising their own publicity stunts and monitoring their own sales. Labour turnover has improved considerably. Supervisors have been dispensed with now that everyone is accountable directly to the branch manager. Yet there are boundaries around the extent of the decision-making. Staff teams do not devise their own menus, decide on prices or change the company logo.

Harvester teams meet regularly to suggest improvements, which sounds a lot like those other once-fashionable terms, Total Quality Management (TQM) and quality circles. TQM involves examining and improving the quality of a product or service at every stage of the process, rather than inspecting it for faults at the end. This can only be done by involving (that

Box 10.2 continued

word again!) all employees at every stage of the process. All are expected to contribute to improving quality, no matter what their job. It is a slow process, through small, incremental changes known as 'continuous improvement'. It is not a quick fix. Quality circles are team meetings designed to discuss quality and are one element in the total quality process.

Some organizations attempt to turn themselves into 'learning organizations', another vogue concept. Learning organizations encourage employees to apply the continuous improvement concept to themselves as individuals, so that they learn, grow and develop for themselves and for the organization. A more recent idea is 'business process reengineering', designed to break down barriers between different departments and cut out unnecessary intermediate steps in the production process.

Whether these movements are fads or major conceptual breakthroughs in improving the way we work, they are all part of a drive to use people's talents, energy and time more effectively. Some are inspired by the view that people should have fulfilling work lives. Others are a thinly disguised means of getting more work done with less people. They all can help an organization become more competitive.

Where empowerment is the aim on a much wider scale, there is usually a single theme, most often total quality management (TQM) or continuous improvement (see Box 10.2). The introduction is usually accompanied by training for all, and here the dilemma described earlier is apparent again. If the leader wishes to empower everyone and demonstrate this by arranging company-wide training, what message does compulsory training send to the workforce? Certainly not one of being empowered to decide whether to attend. Induction and training are usually implemented top down on the basis that no one can be empowered unless their boss 'allows' it. This again implies a dependence which does not align with true empowerment, though there is obvious advantage in senior people 'walking the talk'.

WHAT HELPS AND HINDERS EMPOWERMENT?

Some important factors helping or hindering the success of an empowerment initiative are the reward system, organizational support, organization structure and what happens when someone makes a mistake.

Reward systems

One of the most important aspects of introducing empowerment is the need to look at *reward systems*, both formal and informal. If 'old style' behaviour is what attracts the greater rewards, employees are unlikely to behave differently. For example, in a production environment where pay is based on volume produced, there is little sense in empowering the line operatives to stop the line when a *quality* problem arises. Quantity is what gets rewarded. It is evident that producing quality products needs to yield the greater rewards. Failure to take full account of reward systems is often the main cause of failure of an empowerment initiative.

Less formal rewards than pay can be harder to detect or predict. One example of this arose in a heavy engineering company. Parts had to be dipped in a tank to remove machining lubricant before passing on for further fabrication. The cleaning fluid was expensive and the tank large. In the past the fluid had been renewed once a week. It was not uncommon for complex fabrications to be rejected many stages down the line because of faulty cleaning at the cleansing tank and this obviously involved much wasted time and money. Analysis showed that cost savings could be achieved by earlier change of the fluid on occasions, but this could not be done on a routine basis. A decision was made that the tank operator should be encouraged and supported in making the decision. He was in fact confident about this, and said that he had often thought the present system was stupid. Simply watching for a surface film to become visible was sufficient to indicate that change was needed. There seemed to be no problems. The tank operator proved to be very skilled at judging when the fluid needed changing. Sometimes this occurred in well under one week while at other times the fluid was clean enough for much longer.

Unfortunately, the time it took to empty, clean and refill the tank was nearly 30 minutes and the operators down the line from the tank were soon protesting and demanding a return to the old system. While no one was paid on production rate, the bonus did rise as work in progress fell and the disruption to production caused by the unplanned nature of the fluid changes sometimes increased work in progress. The tank operator was put under tremendous pressure to decide on fluid changes only at the end of each day.

A great deal of consultation had taken place, the skill needed had been taken into account, the financial analysis had been performed and there was general support for the change. Rejected work was dramatically reduced, considerable sums of money were saved yet no one had foreseen the consequences of the irregular changes in fluid.

A very positive example in the public sector illustrates two ways in which one form of empowerment was encouraged and rewarded at an organization level as well as for specific individuals. The organization was largely funded for and occupied in conducting tasks for central government and other parts of the public sector. A decision was made at the higher level to encourage entrepreneurial behaviour within some clearly defined parameters relating to confidentiality, exclusivity and quality. Each department was able to keep half of the income generated, to use in reinvesting in a range of different activities, with the remaining half being returned to the Treasury. This was a powerful incentive and some exciting commercial projects were undertaken. Some of the income generated in one department was invested in further development of staff, which in turn equipped them to undertake different commercial work. The second 'reward' for successful empowerment came when the head of the department which had been particularly successful was promoted and moved to head up a whole division. It was also disseminated widely that both entrepreneurial outlook and the individual's determination and support for staff development had been important factors in the promotion. This was unusual – both the criteria for promotion and the publication of reasons for the decision.

Organizational support

Very clear *organization support* is crucial for successful implementation and sustainability. Senior managers must take genuine interest in progress or in the new attitudes and behaviours of the workforce. This support must be visible to all concerned.

Failure can occur when a policy decision overrides the wishes or actions of an empowered workforce. This tests managerial resolve and commitment. One example of this involved the process of filling, sealing, capping and packing a household product. When anything went wrong on the line, a large number of products continued to be produced while someone went to find a supervisor in the large production area who would decide whether the problem was severe enough to stop the line. As part of an empowerment initiative, the operators were given responsibility for deciding when to stop the line and were given the means of monitoring production against orders. Appropriate training was provided. All went as planned for many weeks. Then the operators looked at the records they had kept as part of their own initiative. They discovered that almost all the line stoppages arose using one supplier's materials whereas the other supplier's goods caused virtually no problems at all. The operators suggested that the company moved to a single supplier. This was turned down as 'against company policy', yet the company took no action to get the second supplier to improve. The problem continued, the operators became disillusioned, quality began to drop back and output was wasted. A clear case of leaders failing to act on the recommendations of the newly empowered workforce.

Organizational structure

Another condition for successful empowerment concerns *organization structure*. Empowerment generally works well at the most senior levels and at the most junior levels. The middle levels often resist change and hang on to their areas of responsibility by any means available to them. This is one reason why empowerment is often accompanied by delayering. In one company, supervisors were retained and given considerable training, including knowledge and understanding of company strategy, in order to be able to make decisions on a broader front. They proceeded to use this great knowledge as power and were more controlling of the workforce rather than more empowering.

Other areas where inappropriate structure can discourage or derail empowerment involve duplication. For example, where the workforce is given responsibility for quality control, yet quality inspectors or quality control specialists are retained, the operators know that their own checking is going to be double checked. This devalues their contribution, which in turn discourages empowerment on quality issues.

Mistakes

Perhaps most of all, management's behaviour when someone *makes a mistake* within the scope of this empowerment is likely to affect empowerment significantly. Blame or punishment, however informal, are likely to be very detrimental. Skilled leaders can support empowerment by underlining that some mistakes are inevitable, while also encouraging openness about mistakes and using them as opportunities to learn.

A LEADER'S ROLE IN EMPOWERMENT

A leader may be the managing director of a large company, the general manager of one division, the works manager of a small works or the supervisor of a clerical department. The primary requirement is either acceptance of the plan from other more senior people or sufficient independence to make acceptance by others unnecessary. Whatever the circumstances or scope of the desired empowerment, some prerequisites exist for any successful leadership.

Respect and belief

Leaders need to possess genuine respect for the abilities and the potential of staff in their area. They may see untapped potential or ability being used outside work or in other activities, such as in sports teams or the canteen committee. They see strengths as well as weaknesses, and often see the strengths as the route to greater success rather than concentrating on weaknesses as stumbling blocks.

Where this respect is absent, the workforce behave accordingly. In one large catering establishment, there were a number of unskilled jobs which were performed by people with very little education who could neither read nor write. Their supervisor treated them as though they couldn't think for themselves and gave very precise instructions, such as where each item should be stored and in which order jobs should be performed. Yet when an outside consultant involved them in working on ways to improve both performance and job satisfaction, their level of knowledge about health and safety and hygiene surprised everyone. The quality and practicality of their suggestions were a revelation to all. They had not ventured to put forward ideas before because they knew that no one would stop to listen.

Leader's confidence

If leaders are fearful for their own role or their future, they are unlikely to empower their workforce as this might threaten their survival. A successful empowering leader is either willing to take the risk of becoming redundant, accepting the consequences, or is confident of finding a new role. In the most successful cases, a leader continually challenges the workforce to take more and more responsibility within their own area of experience, freeing up time for the leader to take on new tasks or a more future-oriented role.

Training, encouragement and employee confidence

A leader who sets out to empower his or her staff walks a tightrope between respecting the existing ability of staff and making training available to develop latent potential. As with most aspects of empowerment, the successful leader will find a way of involving the workforce in this dilemma, empowering them to look at their own training and development needs. The risk is that the leader will reduce the workforce's confidence by giving them a task which they find too unfamiliar to tackle. The aim is to build confidence, not undermine it. This difficulty can usually be overcome by working with concrete issues. An agenda for a team meeting might consist of the questions: What frustrates you when doing your job? What helps you to do a good job? What gets in the way of doing a better job? What would you like to change about your job? What would you need to make this possible? An empowering leader does not have all the answers, and is willing to say so. He or she is also able to encourage staff to build on what has been suggested, is patient and avoids making rapid judgements as to what is useful or workable.

The leader may need to coach the workforce in new aspects of their role. This can result in a demonstration of power or superiority and thus anti-empowerment. If the knowledge and experience exists within the workforce, finding ways of drawing upon this may be preferable. The manner in which coaching is carried out, by sharing knowledge and experience and encouraging others to make it their own, is a mark of a successful developer. In many situations approaches to development, which enable each person to learn at their own rate and in their preferred way, will be most successful (e.g. computer-based learning, videos, reading, etc.).

Defining the boundaries

When a leader sets out to empower staff, no one imagines that staff will have the freedom to do anything they want. The organization clearly has a strategy which is likely to be determined at a senior level. So a workforce which seeks investment on a production line for a product which is not actively marketed is going to be disappointed. Clarity about the boundary is important.

Empowerment is very unlikely to happen quickly. It may gradually become more evident as the number of people practising an empowered style of working increases and as staff take on wider responsibility and decision-making. Thus, giving a group scope to find its own areas for decision-making is more important than ensuring the size of this scope. Successful empowerers make space for staff to take on responsibility rather than giving it to employees.

Information and communications

When a workforce is empowered to make more decisions, this is usually accompanied by a need for more information. This may involve accurate knowledge of orders outstanding, possible delaying factors or information about key accounts. As in the previous section, a key to successful empowerment is finding a highly involving way in which the workforce can specify their own information needs, including content, timing and who they want to get it. As information is often a symbol of power, this may be much more difficult than it at first appears. Supposed 'reasons' for not sharing information, such as confidentiality, abound in organizations.

Rate of progress

Perhaps this is the most difficult aspect of empowerment for a leader who genuinely wishes to achieve progress. The line between empowering and pushing staff is very fine. Many staff will be very cautious and may be fearful of making mistakes and of the attendant consequences. An attitude that mistakes are learning opportunities is difficult to achieve when anticipating and avoiding mistakes is obviously preferable. Ensuring that blame is not part of the process is critically important if progress is to be sustained and regression avoided.

Rates of progress will depend on history. A new leader has many advantages over a leader who wishes to change his or her style of leadership. An environment where job security is not a major concern is likely to be more fruitful ground, as is a situation where staff are broadly able and confident in their existing roles. A leader who has several different teams or groups of staff is faced with a decision on whether to start empowering the whole workforce at the same time or to choose an area where success is most likely. Listening, encouraging, coaching and patiently building on small successes is usually the best way to proceed.

SUMMARY

This chapter has made plain that the process of empowerment is much more than a leader simply passing on part of his or her task for a subordinate to carry out. It is a philosophy of management that involves giving more responsibility and decision-making opportunities to those lower down the organization. The main objective is to enable decisions to be made by those closest to the actual work. This encourages initiative and motivation. Whilst there are many advantages of empowerment, there are factors which can hinder its success. Not least of these are leaders failing to take account of rewards systems. Policy decisions may also override the wishes or actions of the empowered workforce. Leaders seeking to implement a process of empowerment need to take these factors into account if empowerment is to be a success.

11 *Women leaders*

ARE WOMEN LEADERS DIFFERENT FROM MEN LEADERS?

Up until the present time, leadership has often been dominated by men. However, some writers have argued that things might well change in the near future. The reason for this is that there are some suggestions that women may find it easier to be transformational leaders than do men. If women are more transformational than men, and if it is important to be transformational as well as transactional, then does it not follow that women are more effective leaders than men? Or are these assumptions falling into the trap of gender-stereotyping? Certainly, there are other writers who have argued that there are no, or very few, significant differences in the ways that men and women lead.

This chapter will examine some of the arguments for and against the presence of differences between the sexes and attempt to answer the questions: Are women leaders different from men? If they are, are they more effective?

WOMEN LEAD IN DIFFERENT WAYS FROM MEN

Rosener (1990) conducted a survey sent to all members of the International Women's Forum (an organization of prominent women leaders from around the world). Each respondent was asked to name a male leader with similar responsibilities in a similar organization, who received the same questionnaire. Based on the results of her survey, Rosener is convinced that women leaders are more trans-formational and that they are succeeding because of, not in spite of, characteristics generally considered to be 'feminine'. The first female executives, she maintains, had to adopt the style and habits that had proved successful for men. Now a second wave of women is making its way into top management – not by aping men, but by drawing on the skills and attitudes they have developed from their experience as women.

BOX 11.1 YES, WOMEN LEADERS ARE DIFFERENT

The most successful styles of leadership are more closely associated with women than men.

Beverly Alimo-Metcalfe

Women leaders make efforts to encourage participation and share power and information. They do not covet formal authority, having learned to lead without it.

Judy Rosener

Women avoid confrontation at work to achieve consensus through persuasion and compromise.

Spencer Stuart & Associates Ltd

Women managers are more transformational as well as more effective and satisfying as leaders.

Bernard Bass and Bruce Avolio

When questioned about their leadership performance and how they influenced those with whom they worked, the men were more likely to describe themselves in ways that characterize transactional leadership. They viewed their job performance as a series of transactions, exchanging rewards for good performance or punishment for poor performance. The men were also more likely to use power arising from their position.

The women, on the other hand, described themselves in ways that characterize transformational leadership – getting subordinates to transform their own self-interest into the interest of the group, so that personal and organizational goals are linked. They were concerned with consensus building, encouraging participation, being open and inclusive and building up a feeling of self-worth with co-workers and subordinates. The women were more likely to use personal characteristics such as charisma and interpersonal skills rather than their positional power.

However, linking transformational leadership *directly* with being female is a mistake, as Rosener points out. Many women have successfully adopted the transactional style of leadership and prefer that style. Many men successfully use the transformational style of leadership. Even when women leaders use the transformational style, they have to be comfortable using other leadership styles. Sometimes participatory management may be inappropriate, either because of time constraints or because some subordinates may simply prefer to be told what to do and want no part in the decision-making process. Some subordinates may even interpret consultation as uncertainty or a sign of weakness. Leaders, whether men or women, have to be flexible.

WOMEN MAY MAKE BETTER LEADERS

As we have seen earlier, Bass and Avolio (1990) found that although transactional leaders could be good managers, employees are most productive and satisfied when their leaders add to the transactions with transformational behaviour. Transformational leaders develop subordinates to higher levels of potential. They also found that women were rated by subordinates as being more transformational as well as more effective and satisfying as leaders (Bass and Avolio 1992).

One possible explanation for this is that the women were simply of a higher calibre than the men. They had to be, or they would not have reached comparable positions of responsibility. A second possibility is that subordinates have higher expectations of their male leaders and that they may have judged their female leaders more leniently. A third explanation, favoured by Bass and Avolio, is that as women tend to be more nurturing, interested in others and socially sensitive, they display qualities more in line with transformational leadership. This in turn makes them more effective. Men are more likely to practise management-by-exception, that is, intervening only when something goes wrong. They are more likely to monitor the failings of subordinates. Women are more likely to care about them as individuals.

Table 11.1 Masculine versus feminine modes of leadership

Qualities exhibited by male leaders	Qualities exhibited by female leaders
Competitiveness	Cooperativeness
Hierarchical authority	Collaboration of managers and subordinates
High control for the leader	Lower control for the leader
Unemotional, analytical problem-solving	Problem-solving based on intuition and empathy as well as rationality

Source: Adapted from Loden (1985).

Other authors also maintain that women leaders are different from men. Loden (1985) maintained that there is a masculine and a feminine style of leadership as defined by the qualities listed in Table 11.1. Grant (1988) contended that women should stop trying to emulate traditionally male qualities, such as independence and competitiveness, and instead place greater emphasis on traditionally female qualities such as cooperativeness and nurturing.

DIFFERENCES, IF ANY, ARE SMALL

Other researchers reject the notion of gender-stereotypic leadership styles, or at least maintain that the differences are slight. Any differences may be smaller than between, say, managers of big and small companies, or managers of new and old companies, or between one man, or woman, and another.

The basic flaw in Rosener's research, according to Fuchs Epstein (1991), is that Rosener asked the leaders to describe their own leadership styles rather than observing them at work. Fuchs Epstein maintains that men and women tend to stereotype their own behaviour and describe themselves in ways which are seen as gender-appropriate. In other words, men are more likely to describe themselves in 'masculine'/command and control terms. Women are more likely to describe themselves in 'feminine'/transformational terms. Fuchs Epstein gives an example from her own research on women attorneys. One lawyer described herself as 'caring', while a

BOX 11.2 NO, WOMEN LEADERS ARE NOT SO DIFFERENT

The category is 'people', not 'men and women'.

Cynthia Fuchs Epstein

There are greater differences between the way one man manages and another man manages than there are between men and women as groups.

George Bain

Gender differences are sexy, in part because sex is sexy, so we notice them more than other, larger differences.

Jane Mansbridge

There is little reason to believe that either women or men make superior managers, or that women and men are different types of managers.

Gary Powell

---

male colleague described her as a 'barracuda'. Who knows which description was right? Perhaps they both were, and the lawyer was caring, or not, according to the situation. However, the self-description criticism could not be levelled at the Bass and Avolio (1992) research described above. Their findings were based on data collected from ratings by subordinates of male and female leaders on their leader's behaviour.

AN OVERVIEW

Perhaps the most comprehensive report to date on this controversial issue is that by Eagly and Johnson (1990). They examined 162 studies in which there were comparisons between male and female leaders. The results of the studies were analysed by meta-analysis, a statistical method of evaluating the effects of one or more variables across several different studies. Eagly and Johnson found that results differed according to the type of study and according to the style of leadership examined.

Interpersonally-oriented versus task-oriented style

Where leadership behaviour was assessed at the place of work (called *organizational studies*), women appeared no more interpersonally oriented than men, and men appeared no more task oriented than women. It would seem that organizational roles are more important than gender roles and that selection criteria and organizational culture minimize tendencies for leaders to behave in a stereotypic manner. On the other hand, where data were collected from people not at their place of work (called *laboratory studies* and *assessment studies*) there were gender differences.

The strongest evidence that there are differences between men and women occurred when examining democratic and autocratic styles of leadership. Eagly and Johnson showed that women tend to be more democratic or participative in style, whereas men tend to be more autocratic or directive. This tendency was apparent in the organizational studies as well as in the laboratory and assessment studies. This difference between the sexes may reflect the fact that women have superior social and interpersonal skills which enable them to be more adept in the give-and-take of collaborative decision-making. Another possibility is that, as women leaders often encounter negative attitudes about women's competence and status as managers, a participative style of leadership enables them to win acceptance from others. Collaborative decision-making may also increase their own self-confidence.

Presence and absence of gender differences

Eagly and Johnson are often quoted, both by supporters of the view that men and women leaders are different and by supporters of the view that they are not. In answer to the question posed at the beginning of this chapter as to whether women are different to men, the answer seems to be that in some respects, yes, they are. They tend to be more democratic and participative. In other respects, no, they are not. When assessed in an organizational setting, they appear to be no more interpersonally oriented and no less task oriented than men.

As to the question of whether women are more effective than men, Eagly and Johnson do not argue that being more democratic and participative is either an advantage or a disadvantage for women. On the contrary, they acknowledge that both democratic and autocratic styles can be effective according to circumstances. However, they note that traditional, hierarchical management practices have been criticized in recent years and that there have been many advocates for change towards the democratic and participative styles of leadership. Their meta-analysis suggests that these styles are more prevalent among women.

PERCEPTIONS OF MASCULINE AND FEMININE TRAITS

We have seen in the first part of this chapter that there are opposing views as to whether or not there are significant differences between male and female leaders. Nevertheless, the fact that differences are perceived to exist is significant in itself. It has positive and negative implications for women and for men.

If 'masculine' characteristics, such as aggressiveness and authoritarianism are seen as positive traits, for example in a traditional, hierarchical organization, then the more gentle, democratic style perceived as 'feminine' might be seen as a weakness. The perceived difference between the sexes, whether real or not, could result in discrimination against women. On the other hand, if a transformational style of leadership is favoured by an organization and women are perceived to have more of the qualities associated with this style, then the perceived difference could result in discrimination against men.

Whether differences between men and women's behaviour as leaders are actual or perceived, there is no disputing the fact that there are many more men than women in senior executive positions. So two further questions present themselves: Why are there more men than women in senior management? What can be done to redress the balance?

THE STATISTICS

There are many studies showing that women are not making as many inroads on senior positions as might be expected. For example, a study of 200 top companies by Ashridge Management College (Holton *et al.*, 1993) shows that three-quarters of boards of directors are still all-male preserves. Although the number of women board directors has more than doubled since 1989 (from 11 per cent in 1989 to 25 per cent in 1993), out of 51 women on the boards surveyed, only 11 are executive directors (see Figure 11.1).

A similar picture emerges when one looks at the number of

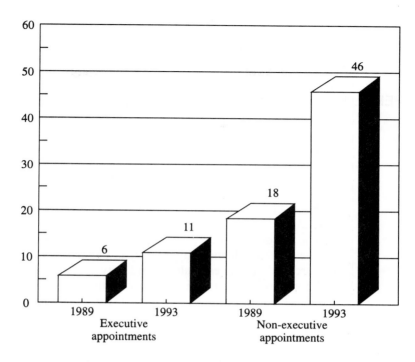

Figure 11.1 Women directors: number of appointments
Source: Adapted from Ashridge Management College survey (Holton *et al.*, 1993).

women on trade union national executives. For example, women make up 68 per cent of the membership of the UK's largest union, Unison, which embraces public services, yet only 20 per cent of the senior national officials are women. The union has set a target to ensure that women make up between 30 per cent and 40 per cent of its senior management before the end of the century. Women currently make up around 36 per cent of the national executive of the general union, the GMB, which is a higher percentage than many other unions.

There are many views as to why there are comparatively few women in senior management. Anita Roddick, founder of Body Shop International, gives one view in Box 11.3. Other explanations include the glass ceiling, the glass house dilemma and the selection barrier.

BOX 11.3 A WOMAN'S PLACE

Despite the great strides that women have made in recent years, we are still second-class citizens in many areas of business and the top echelons of industry are still closed to women. How many women are there in senior positions in engineering or the petrochemical industry? How many women bank managers are there? Precious few.

With more media interest and more media exposure it might seem, superficially, that women in business are rapidly achieving true equality. But I do not believe that women have a chance in hell of achieving their deserved status and power in business within the foreseeable future. My daughters might see it, but I won't.

The reason is that corporations are largely created by men, for men, often influenced by military or public school models. Hierarchical structures built on authority remain unchanged, and many men find it difficult to accept the rise of women to top management positions – perhaps because they have never learned to deal with women other than as secretaries, wives, girlfriends, mothers or adjuncts to themselves.

Male-dominated cultures set up difficult hurdles for women. Much business is conducted in formal and informal clubs, from which women are usually excluded, and criteria for promotion are based on male values. Women have to keep proving themselves by a process of constant education, whereas men can still earn a living in their fifties on skills acquired in their early twenties.

Source: Quoted from Anita Roddick, *Body and Soul*, London, Ebury Press, 1991.

THE GLASS CEILING

No discussion about women leaders can fail to mention the glass ceiling. It is a graphic description of the barriers that prevent women moving up to senior management level, barriers which are so subtle as to be almost invisible and yet are at the same time so strong as to be virtually impenetrable.

One possible explanation for the creation of the glass ceiling is that women are held back by a bias towards the idea that the 'good manager' is male or masculine (Schein, 1973, 1975). Another hypothesis, supported by the findings of Jayson and Williams (1986), is that organizational policies and practices have systematically discriminated against women. Examples of such practices are lack of opportunity and power, tokenism, shortage of mentors and lack of access to challenging and developing assignments.

In their book *Breaking the Glass Ceiling*, Morrison *et al.* (1987) reported on a study of top female executives. This study aimed to find out what factors contributed to success and to failure, whether these factors were the same for women as for men, and whether women needed different development opportunities than men. The key findings are summarized in Table 11.2.

Table 11.2 Key factors identified by top female executives

Six factors for success

1 Help from above (mentor)
2 Track record
3 Desire to succeed
4 Ability to manage subordinates
5 Willingness to take career risks
6 Ability to be tough, decisive and demanding

Three factors for failure

1 Inability to adapt
2 Wanting too much (self or other women)
3 Performance problems

Four factors for career progression

1 Acceptance by the organization
2 Support and encouragement
3 Training and development
4 Challenging work and visible assignments

Source: Adapted from Morrison *et al.* (1987).

Although many of the success and failure factors shown in Table 11.2 apply to both men and women, it appears that, to be successful, women have to have more of the assets and fewer of the liabilities than men. They must have an outstanding track record and be totally competent and dedicated to the organization. They must be able to manage subordinates, especially men, and they must be tough and demanding. They must also be willing to take risks.

The women in the study identified important areas of help for women in their attempt to move up the organization, such as support and encouragement, and training and development. However, many of the women in the study felt that there were limits to how much further they could go. It would seem that even for highly successful women, the glass ceiling is still firmly in position.

THE GLASS HOUSE DILEMMA

Not only do many women leaders face the glass ceiling, but they may feel the effects of the glass house dilemma (Morrison *et al.*, 1986). Because the number of women in top positions in organizations is generally small, many of them feel that they are being scrutinized. They feel that they are judged more harshly than men and that their mistakes may jeopardize not only their own future but the future opportunities of other women within the organization. Thus the tremendous expectations put on successful women leaders can lead to fear of failure and a subsequent reluctance to take risks. The importance to success of being prepared to take risks has been discussed above. It appears that the challenge for women leaders is to break out of the glass house as well as to shatter the glass ceiling.

THE SELECTION BARRIER

There is a suggestion that women may face a barrier at the selection stage; the closed door, as well as the ceiling, may be made of glass. It is against the Sex Discrimination Act to ask women loaded, gender-biased questions at a selection interview. However, if discriminatory questions are asked of women (or men) at interviews, they can at least be picked up by the interviewees and used as evidence of sex discrimination in a court or tribunal. Other means of selection may have more insidious forms of discrimination embedded within them. Even if the hidden bias is unintentional, it is still discriminatory. Alban-Metcalfe (1989), in evaluating the use of assessment centres in a large public sector organization, identified potential concerns, some of which have implications for women's career development.

The first stage of an assessment centre design is the identification of criteria for job success, taken from job incumbents and their bosses. These criteria are then used as a basis for designing exercises and simulations in the assessment process. Since people in the most senior positions are more likely to be male than female, the identified characteristics of successful leaders used in the assessment could be gender-based and therefore potentially biased against women (Alimo-Metcalfe, 1993).

WHAT CAN BE DONE TO REDRESS THE BALANCE?

It appears that positive action is needed if the balance of male and female senior executives is to be redressed.

An example of such positive action is *Opportunity 2000*, a programme launched as a result of work by the Women's Development Target Team and set up by the UK organization Business in the Community in October 1991. The aim of *Opportunity 2000* is to encourage companies to take up the equal opportunities challenge and to create a more balanced workforce.

The NHS is one organization which has taken up this challenge. The NHS is staffed mainly by women, but run mainly by men. As part of *Opportunity 2000*, the health service aims to increase its proportion of female general managers from 18 per cent in 1991 to 30 per cent by 1994. Positive discrimination in selection is illegal, but positive action, such as providing particular training and development opportunities for women, is not. In order to reach the targets set, the NHS has embarked upon a programme of specialized training for potential women executives in order to give them the skills needed to break the NHS glass ceiling.

One of the six factors of success listed in Table 11.2 was 'help from above (mentor)'. Mentors are usually older, successful colleagues who offer advice to less experienced employees and enhance their personal development. They also bring their protégés to the notice of top management, which is a vital step in gaining career advancement. Many writers agree that mentors are crucial, especially for women. They often have to battle against a traditional, masculine, organizational culture and may have more barriers to overcome than men. They see few other women in top executive positions. To be helped and advised by successful, more experienced employees of power and status has proved to be of great assistance to women in climbing the organizational ladder.

Most women are still expected to bear the responsibility of managing the home and the welfare of children. There are many things which organizations can do to *facilitate the dual role of women*. They can try to limit the amount of travel expected, for example, or provide on-site crèche facilities. Many companies in recent years have introduced flexitime. All such facilities can help women break the glass ceiling and at the same time make conditions easier for male employees as well. Further details of this interesting issue, as well as other equal opportunity matters, including *Opportunity 2000*, can be found in another book in this series (Newell, 1995).

SUMMARY

Opinion varies among writers and researchers as to whether there are significant differences between women and men leaders. One argument is that traditionally female qualities such as nurturing and social sensitivity result in a tendency for women leaders to be more transformational than their male counterparts. Other researchers state that differences, if any, are slight and warn against gender stereotyping. It does seem, however, that women tend to display a more democratic or participative style of leadership and men tend to be more autocratic or directive. What is not in dispute is that, although the situation is changing, there are still more men in senior executive positions than women. Women may find themselves up against the 'glass ceiling', unable to penetrate the barrier which prevents them moving up into senior management positions. Initiatives such as *Opportunity 2000*, mentoring and flexible working conditions, more conducive to juggling work and family responsibilities, aim to redress the balance.

12 *Leadership across frontiers*

A CASE IN POINT

In 1980, a middle management acquaintance of the author from a large organization in England travelled to the Far East to work for a period of two years with a similar organization in Hong Kong. He was an experienced, popular and effective supervisor in his own organization and the intention was that he would bring some of his work experience and managerial expertise to the organization abroad. He was accompanied by his wife and family, provided with accommodation and a temporary guide, and given time to adjust to the local conditions. He had all the equipment and resources he would need to do the job there. Expectations were high on all sides.

Within a few months it started to become clear that something was going wrong with the arrangement. Although all of his new staff were able to speak English fluently, it was apparent that the new supervisor was unable to communicate with them effectively nor they with him. He felt that he was just not getting his ideas across. For their part, they felt that he didn't understand or care about their culture or way of working. Performance within the particular section soon started to deteriorate and dissatisfaction and resentment began to set in. By the end of six months things had become so bad that it was clear that the situation could not be allowed to continue. After meetings with senior management, the contract was cancelled and the expatriate supervisor and his family returned to England. What might have been a useful and constructive experience had proved to be a frustrating, expensive and time-consuming failure for all concerned.

So, what went wrong? Why, after all of the arrangements and

careful planning, was the venture not successful? Was it something to do with the personalities of the parties involved? Could it have been the particular leadership style of the expatriate supervisor? If that was the case, then why had his style worked in England but not in Hong Kong? Can the leadership styles of one culture be transported and operate effectively in another culture? In this chapter we will try to answer these and other similar questions.

WHAT IS CULTURE?

Hofstede (1991) suggests that culture is the collective programming of the mind which distinguishes the members of one group or society from those of another. It is reflected in the group's particular assumptions, perceptions, thought patterns, norms and values. National cultural values are formed as boundaries encourage interaction and socialization within certain regions or countries. National cultural differences can be found rooted in fundamental values and beliefs, and these can be reflected in different patterns of behaviour which are found in different countries. However, the movement of people across boundaries and the changing of frontiers, together with differences in social and economic experience, mean that different layers of culture, and also sub-cultures, can exist in all countries.

To emphasize this, Trompenaars (1993) points to the fact that his research has shown that there are, at several levels, as many differences between the cultures of West Coast and East Coast America, as there are between different nations. This fact illustrates one of the major problems in distinguishing different cultures: how to draw boundaries between cultures. How much difference, for example, must there be between two populations before we can say that they are different cultures?

Clearly then, there are difficulties in identifying and classifying different cultural groups. Because of this, it is intended in this chapter to refer to distinctions between different cultures by means of 'national culture' or the general culture of the country to which we refer. In doing this, however, it is important to bear in mind that, as in the case of the East and West Coasts of America, within any major nation of the world there can be great cultural variation. Also, in considering national cultural differences and comparing cultures, it is important to avoid what is known as the 'ecological fallacy'. That is the mistaken idea that because two cultures differ, then any two members of those cultures must necessarily also differ in the same manner. Obviously this is most unlikely.

CULTURAL DIFFERENCES IN SOCIETY: THE CASE OF OBEDIENCE TO AUTHORITY

Smith and Bond (1993) have investigated cultural differences between nations by comparing the results of studies of social psychology carried out in one country, with replicated studies in another. They have taken nine of the best-known classic North American studies and reviewed what happened when the same studies were repeated in other countries. These studies cover social phenomena such as 'the effects of exposure to a stimulus', 'social loafing', 'conformity and obedience', 'leadership', 'group decision-making' and 'group conflict and cooperation'. The review of the findings from the studies clearly demonstrates that processes such as self-perception, communication, conformity, leadership and decision-making, all occur differently in cultural groups according to how collective or individualistic they are.

To illustrate this, one of the classic studies Smith and Bond looked at was Milgram's (1963) study of obedience to authority, which is one of the most controversial and widely discussed studies in social psychology. In this study, Milgram found that 65 per cent of his American subjects accepted orders to give continuing electric shocks to other people, even though it was clearly visible that each shock was stronger than the last and that in some cases the supposed 'victims' were screaming and near to collapse. (The 'victims' were, in fact, confederates of the experimenter and were not actually receiving electric shocks.) This study has been repeated with minor variations in at least eight other countries.

The results of all of the obedience studies carried out are shown in Table 12.1. It can be seen from this that the percentage obedience rate varies as widely as from 16 per cent for females in Australia, to 92 per cent for the general population in Holland. The obedience rates shown refer to the percentage of subjects who continued to administer shocks right up to the maximum level of 450 volts. (In the Italian study the maximum shock level was only 330 volts.) The Australians and British were found to be less obedient than the Americans, Germans, Dutch, Italians, Austrians and Spanish. On the

Table 12.1 Studies of destructive obedience to authority

Country	Subject	Percentage obedient
USA	Male general population	65
USA	Female general population	65
USA	Students	85
UK	Male students	50
Spain	Students	Over 90
Jordan	Students	62
Italy	Students	85
Holland	General population	92
Germany	Male general population	85
Austria	General population	80
Australia	Male students	40
Australia	Female students	16

Source: Adapted from Smith and Bond (1993).

surface then, it would appear that there might be cultural differences in relation to obedience to carrying out orders.

Of course, many differences may also have contributed to the variation in results obtained, such as samples studied or methods used. For this reason, Smith and Bond suggest that a more useful way to learn from this batch of studies is to examine what factors caused changes in levels of obedience *within* each country, and then compare these results *across* countries. One such factor identified is the presence of another person during the experiment.

In Milgram's (1974) American study, when extra accomplices refused to carry out their part in administering shocks, the percentage obedience fell from 65 per cent to 10 per cent, in Holland from 92 per cent to 16 per cent and in Germany from 85 per cent to a still comparatively high rate of 52 per cent. Clearly the actions of additional people in the experimental setting can affect obedience levels considerably, but, it appears, more in some cultures than in others. People take into account the social context around them, but the importance of this social context may vary from country to country.

CULTURAL DIFFERENCES AND MANAGEMENT

In research carried out over a period of 15 years, involving 15,000 employees in 50 countries, Trompenaars (1993) has identified four broad types of culture giving rise to four different styles of management. He identifies these as the Family, the Eiffel Tower, the Guided Missile and the Incubator.

The *Family* model is typical of cultures as seemingly disparate as Japan, India, Italy and Spain. These have a very hierarchical power-oriented corporate culture in which the leader is regarded as the caring head of the family. Delegation is difficult because the leader is a father figure who is seen as knowing best for his subordinates. Praise is a better motivator than money. Japanese companies with this type of culture tend to recreate aspects of the traditional family.

The *Eiffel Tower* model is typical of large French companies, and also German and Dutch ones. This is also hierarchical but much more impersonal and rule driven. Each successive level in the hierarchy has a clear and demonstrable function of holding together the levels beneath it to maintain the management structure.

The *Guided Missile* model is so called because it is based on a view of the organization as a missile homing in on strategic objectives and targets. The overriding principle is to do whatever it takes to complete a task or reach a goal. Many American and Swedish companies are typical of this type of organization as, to a lesser extent, are some British companies.

Finally there is the *Incubator* model. Organizations of this type are structured around the fulfilment of individual members' needs and aspirations. The management framework of the organization exists to free employees from routine tasks so they can pursue creative activities. These are typified by the new companies of California's Silicon Valley.

Trompenaar's conclusions from his research contrast starkly with the idea that the world is becoming a 'global village' in which a new generation of international managers will operate easily across borders. Instead, he argues, many companies have found that even their most tried and tested formulae do not travel well. Management techniques from one culture frequently fail in another. For example, performance-related pay, which operates successfully in many cultures, is found not to be accepted in France, Germany and Italy. In these cultures it is frowned upon for individual group members to excel in a way that reveals the shortcomings of other members. Trompenaars believes that in every culture, authority, bureaucracy, creativity, empowerment, verification and accountability are experienced in different ways.

HOFSTEDE'S CLASSIC RESEARCH

Perhaps the most extensive research ever carried out into cultural differences is that reported upon by Hofstede (1980, 1985, 1991). The original research questionnaire was based on 116,000 respondents from more than 50 countries. Questionnaire items concerned various aspects of employees' work experience. The data from this were analysed in such a way as to make comparisons between countries.

From factor analysis of the mean scores, Hofstede was able to classify the countries by means of four cultural dimensions: power distance, uncertainty avoidance, individualism/collectivism and

Table 12.2 Rankings of a sample of national cultures using Hofstede's classification

Country	Power distance	Uncertainty avoidance	Individualism	Masculinity
Arab region	7	27	26	23
Australia	41	37	2	16
Belgium	20	5	8	22
Canada	39	41	4	24
France	15	12	10	35
Germany	43	29	15	9
Great Britain	43	47	3	9
Hong Kong	15	49	37	18
India	10	45	21	20
Ireland	49	47	12	7
Italy	34	23	7	4
Japan	33	7	22	1
Pakistan	32	24	47	25
Singapore	13	53	40	28
Sweden	47	49	10	53
Switzerland	45	33	14	4
United States	38	43	1	15

Source: Adapted from Hofstede (1983).

masculinity/femininity. Table 12.2 shows the rankings of national cultures in relation to these dimensions using Hofstede's classification.

The *power distance* score of a country shows to what extent that country accepts that power is distributed unequally in organizations (Hofstede, 1985). This concerns the amount of respect and difference between those in superior and subordinate positions. People in large power distance cultures have steep hierarchies with more levels of control in which everyone has their proper place. Management style is likely to be paternalistic.

Hofstede found that Belgium, and also countries in Southern Europe such as France, Greece, Italy, Portugal and Spain, had large or medium power distances. Countries with small power distances, such as most of the Northern European countries (Denmark, Finland, Norway, Sweden, Britain, Ireland, Germany and the Netherlands), had flattish hierarchies where bureaucracy was minimized and tasks delegated. Power distance, it seems, goes to the core of management issues and leadership style as it gives an indication of how different levels in the hierarchy relate to each other and how power is wielded.

Hofstede defined *uncertainty avoidance* (UA), as society's fears of the unknown and the extent to which a culture programmes its members to feel either comfortable or uncomfortable in the face of uncertainty and ambiguity. Weak uncertainty avoidance cultures accept uncertainty and let it happen, whilst strong uncertainty avoidance cultures feel uncomfortable with ambiguity and try to control the future. These strong UA cultures tend to be less tolerant of differing views and ideas and have more written rules and regulations, procedures and codes. They respect the value of specialists and experts who can help to reduce uncertainty.

Hofstede's research shows that most Southern European countries, such as France, Greece, Italy, Portugal and Spain and also including Germany, tend to be high on uncertainty avoidance, indicating a desire to control the future and reduce anxiety. This manifests itself in the focus on formal procedures, safety and security measures and long careers in the same business. Sweden, Denmark, Britain and Ireland, on the other hand, are found to be low on uncertainty avoidance. This is expressed by a preference for managers who are outward-going, decisive and practical.

Individuality–collectivism is to do with whether one's identity is defined by personal choices and achievements, or by the character of collective groups to which an individual is permanently attached.

BOX 12.1 AN ANALYSIS OF THE CASE IN POINT

If we look at the rankings of Britain and Hong Kong in relation to Hofstede's four dimensions shown in Table 12.2, we can begin to get some idea of what might have caused at least some of the problems described in the Case in Point at the beginning of this chapter.

Taking power distance, we can see that Hong Kong ranked high at 15, whilst Britain ranked low at 43. This tends to suggest that there are considerable differences between the two cultures in relation to how power is arranged and exercised. Large power distance cultures, such as Hong Kong, have more levels of control in which everyone has their proper place, whilst small power distance cultures, such as Britain, tend to minimize bureaucracy and delegate tasks. In relation to individualism/collectivism, an even greater difference exists between the two cultures. Britain is ranked 3 with Hong Kong ranked 37. This indicates that the two cultures also differ greatly in relation to their emphasis on achievement and their approach to communication and conflict. Individualist societies like Britain prefer direct and open communication and resolving conflict, whilst collectivist cultures prefer harmony and the avoidance of confrontation. The differences on these two dimensions alone suggest that individuals from the two cultures could have difficulty in working together. There is other evidence to support this.

A study by Westwood *et al.* (1992) found that Chinese organizations were characterized by larger power distance arrangements, respect for authority and strict hierarchical arrangements. Chinese executives favoured less assertive, compromising and conflict-avoiding styles. British executives favoured more assertive, collaborating and competing styles.

The results of a few studies cannot fully explain the problems and failure of the situation described in the Case in Point. Personal and dispositional factors may also have played a part. Other managers in similar situations may well adapt successfully. However, the Case in Point and the above studies do illustrate the kinds of problems which can be encountered and which contribute towards the difficulty of transporting leadership across cultures.

Hofstede defines an individualist society as one where emphasis is placed on individual achievement and where everyone is expected to care for themselves and their immediate family only. Collectivist countries are those that have very clear norms and expectations of how people should behave towards each other. They are associated with strong extended family units. Key values include achieving harmony at work, agreement in meetings, and 'face-saving' in work and social situations. 'Face', dignity and harmony in relationships are preferable to over-direct confrontation.

Hofstede's findings show that Britain is ranked as the third highest individualist country world-wide, after the USA and Australia. Nearly all of Western Europe (with the exception of Portugal and Greece) is individualistic. Far Eastern countries (e.g. Korea and Hong Kong but with the exception of Japan) and South-East Asian countries (i.e. Malaysia, Thailand and the Philippines) tend to be more collectivist cultures (see Box 12.1).

The dimension *masculinity–femininity* refers to the extent to which men and women play different roles in the culture. In some cultures men are more dominating, assertive and competitive, whilst women are more modest, caring and nurturing. In such cultures, the norms and values for society as a whole tend to reflect the men's preferences. These cultures are identified by Hofstede as masculine (e.g. Austria, Italy, Britain, Germany). Other cultures, where there is less social differentiation between men and women and where men can take a more modest caring role if they wish, Hofstede labels as feminine (e.g. Denmark, Netherlands, Norway, Sweden and Portugal).

On the masculine–feminine dimension, there are deep differences in attitudes towards business and towards work itself. Masculine cultures such as Britain, Germany and the USA are performance oriented. People tend to be competitive and individuals aim for personal achievement. In feminine cultures, such as Sweden and the Netherlands, solidarity is important. These are welfare oriented, where the strong are expected to help the weak. Some observers have criticized the use of the terms 'masculinity' and 'femininity' as sexist. Also, some have argued that there is a growing 'international business culture' which is closer to the masculine than to the feminine culture. Despite that, the dimension provides a further measure of the differences between cultures.

EVALUATION OF HOFSTEDE'S WORK

There are criticisms of Hofstede's research and identification of cultural differences. One of the main criticisms concerns the sampling of the individuals who were representative of the countries studied. All of the respondents were employees of IBM which has a very distinctive culture. This might have biased the results. However, finding national cultural differences, despite the unifying influence of belonging to the same corporation, can be counted as a strength of Hofstede's research.

A further criticism is that Hofstede's study might be biased towards Western values, simply because it is based on a questionnaire designed by Western researchers. In view of this, research has been carried out by the Chinese Culture Connection (1987), which has investigated Chinese cultural values of Chinese respondents. Analysis of these data yielded four factors, three of which show overlap with Hofstede's dimensions of power distance, individualism–collectivism, and masculinity–femininity. The research also suggested that uncertainty-avoidance and a factor described as *Confucian work dynamism*, are less universally accessible values. Hofstede himself accepts that adding Confucian values to his four dimensions would help to make them more culturally valid.

LOW AND HIGH CONTEXT SOCIETIES

Other researchers have drawn attention to the many differences between cultures and have identified other dimensions. Hall (1959, 1976) and Hall and Hall (1990) for example, have identified *low and high context* societies in relation to language usage. Context refers to the information that surrounds an event. A high context (HC) communication is one in which most of the information is implied or already in the person, and the words spoken will convey only a small part of the message. This can be illustrated by twins who have grown up together and therefore are able to communicate more economically than others who have not. A low context (LC) communication, is just the opposite. Speech is explicit and the message intended is either completely or largely conveyed by the actual words used.

Cultures can be compared on a scale from high to low context. High context cultures, such as Japan, Arab countries and Southern European countries, tend to be more in the know about events than low context cultures. They have developed extensive informal networks for orally exchanging information which is therefore spread more rapidly, albeit unofficially. Low context cultures such as Northern European countries, prefer explicit, clear, written forms of communication as expressed in books and official correspondence.

Hall (1983) also draws attention to the fact that notions of time differ across cultures, and distinguishes cultures which view time monochronically from cultures which view it polychronically. In monochronic societies such as North America and some Northern European countries, punctuality is valued and time is economized. Polychronic societies, on the other hand, are used to doing many things at the same time and do not mind being interrupted. They tend to have a more relaxed view of time. A polychronic view of time sees the maintenance of relationships as the important thing. Low context peoples are generally monochronic whereas high context peoples are generally polychronic.

CROSS-CULTURAL STUDIES OF LEADERSHIP

Empirical research into cultural differences in leadership is comparatively sparse. Yukl (1994) points out that the amount of research on any particular topic of leadership in different cultures is, so far, relatively small, and the methodological difficulties associated with such research are quite large. In addition to obvious language problems, sampling procedures are often inadequate and there are problems in interpreting results due to cultural differences in underlying assumptions about human nature and organizations. Because of this, Yukl believes that it is still too early to draw any firm conclusions about the universal and specific aspects of leadership in different cultures. He suggests that this will be an important area for future leadership research.

Nevertheless, there are studies which provide evidence to support the notion of differences, whilst some of these at the same time provide evidence of cultural similarities. For example, Smith *et al.* (1989) found the distinction between task and relationship behaviour was meaningful in all of the countries included in their research (i.e. Britain, USA, Japan and Hong Kong). However, specific behaviours associated with these broad categories differed across cultures, as did the specific behaviours considered appropriate for managers. From this, the investigators concluded that transcultural dimensions of leader style can be identified but the skill of executing each style effectively varies from culture to culture.

A study by Podsakoff *et al.* (1986) came to broadly similar conclusions. They examined the effectiveness of leader reward and punishment behaviours across a number of different cultures. The findings showed that positive reward behaviour was an important aspect of leadership effectiveness in different cultures, but that the types of behaviour rewarded, and the way rewards were used, were different in many of the cultures.

Laurent (1986) investigated differences in the attitudes and behaviours towards management of middle and senior level managers in a number of European countries. This research suggested that French and Italian managers tend to be more directive and less willing to delegate than Danish and British managers. Another finding by Laurent (1983) showed that French and Italian managers say that they rarely by-pass the hierarchy to achieve work efficiency compared to Danish, British and German managers. Although this can be interpreted as the French and Italians being more conformist and inflexible, Leeds *et al.* (1993) believe that it may reflect conflict-avoiding strategies of French and Italian managers, used to greater power distance, who have a reluctance to admit the prevalence of unofficial practices.

EUROPEAN CULTURAL MAPPING AND LEADERSHIP

Using the dimensions established from research into cultural differences by many researchers, Leeds *et al.* (1993) have analysed the differences between European countries. They believe that on most dimensions, countries are not spaced equally, but instead form clusters where there are marked similarities of behaviour and values related to leadership. Whilst most other researchers tend to group all Western countries together as 'individualist', Leeds *et al.* believe that this is an overgeneralization and that further distinctions can be made. They stress, however, that no one country or cluster group possesses cultural traits which are unique, since traits found in one can also be found in another. Because of this, some of these groups can be viewed as linked as in a series of concentric circles. Leeds *et al.* have identified a total of six European country clusters.

The first cluster comprises the UK and Ireland in Europe but would also include other English-speaking countries outside of

Europe such as the United States, Canada, Australia and New Zealand. These are described as an *Anglo* culture, where leadership is seen as a means of achieving desired outcomes. This culture is underpinned by certain beliefs about people and the nature of organizations which shape and relate its approach to leadership. In Anglo cultures it is believed that wholehearted commitment of followers is achieved through good human relations and communication. Leadership is a means of extending loyalty and commitment.

A second cluster comprises Denmark, Finland, Norway and Sweden, called a *Scandinavian* cluster. This is similar to the Anglo cluster, with which it shares some values and beliefs. However, in one important aspect the Scandinavian cluster is different. This is the concern with the quality of working relationships and with the quality of life, both at work and outside of work. Leadership in Scandinavia is about relationships rather than results, according to Leeds *et al.*

A third cluster is labelled *Latin Mediterranean*. This comprises Italy, Portugal and Spain. These countries have similar values which influence the style, rather than the purpose, of leadership. In this cluster leaders are seen as, and expected to be, more powerful. The power gives them much greater influence over their followers. Followership is less dependent on the results which could be achieved or on the type of relationship created, but is a response to the power of the leader. Leadership in these cultures is less obviously achieved through the leader's own efforts and more through the status of the leader and as a function of his or her position.

Other groupings are Germany with Austria and Switzerland in a *Germanic* cluster; *Northern Latin*, comprising Belgium and France; and *Near Eastern*, comprising Greece, Iran and Turkey. Depending on the dimensions considered, different clusters can be formed. Clusters themselves can also mask differences between cultural groups.

MINIMIZING CULTURE SHOCK

Durcan (1993) believes that for leadership to be effective in one culture, it must meet the needs and expectations of both the followers and leaders in that context. He suggests that to perform similar activities in different conditions is to perform different activities. Also, moving outside of a familiar culture renders an individual temporarily, or occasionally even permanently, illiterate. He points out that there is growing evidence to support the view that simply exporting the models of leadership from one culture to another, either in person or as concepts, is not satisfactory. Leadership models need to fit the cultures in which they are employed.

Does this suggest that a leader from one culture can never succeed in another? Earley (1987) believes that this is not the case. He has shown that people doing business abroad can avoid culture shock, and minimize the chances of offending foreign hosts, by learning about the other culture in advance of their assignments abroad. Earley studied 80 managers employed by an American firm who were due to work for three months in South Korea. Prior to commencing their secondments, one group of managers received training by learning about South Korean culture in a practical, interpersonal approach. A second group trained by reading about the culture in a 'documentary approach'. There were two additional groups: one which received both types of training and another which received no training at all. During the assignment abroad measures were taken of the managers' work effectiveness and difficulty in adjusting to the local culture. The findings showed that those managers receiving both types of training found it much easier to adjust than those receiving just one type of training. Either type of training, however, was more effective than no training at all. These results suggest that training for intercultural assignments can ease the transition into new cultures.

THE TRANSNATIONAL MANAGER

An influential book called *Managing Across Borders* by Bartlett and Ghoshal (1989) suggests that we need to consider cross-border managerial assignments in the context of the way different companies manage their overseas operations. Bartlett and Ghoshal suggest that for world-wide operations, the answer lies in the creation of *transnational companies*. These would be superior to the centralized global structures of many Japanese and American organizations, and also superior to the multinational type structure of many European companies. They believe that success in today's international climate requires a transnational company to disperse around the world, not only its local sales and distribution, but also a degree of its research, design and development. In order to be successful in this, it needs to share internal power between its units around the world instead of maintaining all of the power in the home country. This requires specialized, yet closely linked, groups of managers comprising global business managers, country or regional managers, world-wide functional managers and corporate managers.

The *global business manager*'s job is to serve as a strategist, architect and co-ordinator of the company's transactions across national borders. The main objective is to achieve global scale efficiency and competitiveness. The *country manager*'s job is to be sensitive and responsive to the local market by meeting local needs and satisfying local rules, regulations and procedures. The *functional manager*'s job is to scan for specialized information world-wide and to cross-pollinate knowledge and best practice. Finally, the *corporate manager*'s job is the most vital role in transnational management. This involves leadership and the ability to identify and develop talented, business, country and functional managers, and to balance negotiations between them.

Bartlett and Ghoshal believe that successful corporate managers make the recruitment, training and development of promising executives a top priority. They suggest that a company's ability to identify individuals with potential and integrate them successfully is the single clearest indicator that the corporate leader is a true global manager and that the company itself is a true transnational company.

SUMMARY

So, where does this leave us? We have seen that many cultural differences can exist between different countries and regions and even areas of a country. We have also seen a practical example of the difficulties that can face a leader from one culture adjusting to another culture and the empirical evidence to show what might have caused this. This might lead us to the conclusion that a leader from one culture can never ever operate effectively in another. While many individuals have, and do, make the transition successfully, this transition should never be taken for granted. To be successful, a leadership style which operates effectively in one country will often need to be tailored considerably in order to fit with the culture of another. As global and transnational organizations expand in number and change in form, the demands on the transnational manager to adapt and learn will become an increasing challenge.

— Bibliography

Alban-Metcalfe, B. (1989) *The use of assessment centres in the NHS*, NHS Training Authority Report.

Alimo-Metcalfe, B. (1993) 'Women in management: Organizational socialization and assessment practices that prevent career advancement', *International Journal of Selection and Assessment*, 1, 68–83.

Ashour, A.S. (1973) 'The contingency model of leadership effectiveness: An evaluation', *Organizational Behaviour and Human Performance*, 9, 339–355.

Avolio, B.J. and Bass, B.M. (1991) *Full Range Leadership Development*, Program Manual, New York: State University of New York at Binghamton.

Baron, R.A. and Greenberg, J. (1990) *Behavior in Organizations*, Boston: Allyn & Bacon.

Bartlett, C.A. and Ghoshal, S. (1989) *Managing Across Borders: The Transnational Solution*, London: Century Business, Random House.

Bartlett, C.A. and Ghoshal, S. (1992) 'What is a global manager?', *Harvard Business Review*, Sept./Oct., 124–132.

Bass, B.M. (1954) 'The leaderless group discussion', *Psychological Bulletin*, 51, 465–492.

Bass, B.M. (1985) 'Leadership: Good, better, best', *Organizational Dynamics*, Winter, 26–40.

Bass, B.M. (1990) Editorial: 'Towards a meeting of minds', *Leadership Quarterly*, 1.

Bass, B.M. and Avolio, B.J. (1990) 'Developing transformational leadership: 1992 and beyond', *Journal of European Training*, 14, 21–27.

Bass, B.M. and Avolio, B.J. (1992) 'Shatter the glass ceiling: Women may make better managers', *Center for Leadership Studies Report*, 1, 1–9, New York: SUNY Binghamton.

Bavelas, A., Hastorf, A.H., Gross, A.E. and Kite, W.R. (1965) 'Experiments on the alteration of group structure', *Journal of Experimental Social Psychology*, 1, 55–70.

Bennis, W.G. and Nanus, B. (1985) *Leaders: the Strategies for Taking Charge*, New York: Harper & Row.

Blake, R.R. and Monton, J.S. (1964) *The Managerial Grid*, Houston, Tex.: Gulf Publishing.

Blake, R.R. and McCanse, A.A. (1991) *Leadership Dilemmas: Grid Solutions*, Houston, Tex.: Gulf Publishing.

Block, P. (1987) *The Empowered Manager: Positive Political Skills at Work*, Oxford: Jossey-Bass.

Branson, R. (1985) 'Risk taking', *Journal of General Management*, 11, 5–11.

Brindle, L. (1992) 'Winners and losers in the career stakes', *Human Resources*, Spring, 95–98.

Bryman, A. (1992) *Charisma and Leadership in Organizations*, London: Sage.

Burns, J.M. (1978) *Leadership*, New York: Harper & Row.

Chemers, M.M., Hays, R.B., Rhodewelt, F. and Wysocki, J. (1985) 'A person-environment analysis of job stress: A contingency model explanation', *Journal of Personality and Social Psychology*, 49, 628–635.

Chinese Culture Connection (1987) 'Chinese values and the search for culture-free dimensions of culture', *Journal of Cross-Cultural Psychology*, 18, 143–164.

Conger, J.A. (1989) *The Charismatic Leader: Beyond the Mystique of Exceptional Leadership*, San Francisco: Jossey-Bass.

Conger, J.A. (1990) 'The dark side of leadership', *Organizational Dynamics*, Autumn, 44–55.

Conger, J.A. (1991) 'Inspiring others: The language of leadership', *Academy of Management Executive*, 5, 31–45.

Conger, J.A. and Kanungo, R. (1987) 'Toward a behavioral theory of charismatic leadership in organizational settings', *Academy of Management Review*, 12, 637–647.

Daft, Richard L. (1993) *Management* (3rd edition), Orlando, Fla.: Dryden Press, Harcourt Brace College Publishers.

Dessler, G. and Valenzi, E.R. (1977) 'Initiation of structure and subordinate satisfaction: a path analysis test of path–goal theory', *Academy of Management Journal*, 20, 251–259.

Dobbins, G.H. (1986) 'Equity vs equality: Sex differences in leadership', *Sex Roles*, 15(9–10), 513–525.

Dobbins, G.H. and Russell, J.M. (1986a) 'The biasing effects of subordinate likeableness on leaders' responses to poor performers: A laboratory and field study', *Personnel Psychology*, 39(4), 759–777.

Dobbins, G.H. and Russell, J.M. (1986b) 'Self-serving biases in leadership: A laboratory experiment', *Journal of Management*, 12(4), 475–483.

Durcan, J. (1993) 'Leadership: A question of culture?', *The Ashridge Journal*, December, 9–14.

Eagly, A.H. and Johnson, B.T. (1990) 'Gender and leadership style: A meta-analysis', *Psychological Bulletin*, 108(2), 233–256.

Earley, P.C. (1987) 'Intercultural training for managers: A comparison of documentary and interpersonal methods', *Academy of Management Journal*, 30, 685–698.

Ehrlich, S.B., Meindl, J.R. and Viellieu, B. (1990) 'The charismatic appeal of a transformational leader: An empirical case study of a small, high technology contractor', *Leadership Quarterly*, 1: 229–248.

Fiedler, F.E. (1967) *A Theory of Leadership*, New York: McGraw-Hill.

Field, R.H.G. (1982) 'A test of the Vroom–Yetton normative model of leadership', *Journal of Applied Psychology*, 67, 532–537.

Field, R.H.G. and House, R.J. (1990) 'A test of the Vroom–Yetton model using manager and subordinate reports', *Journal of Applied Psychology*, 75, 362–366.

Fleishman, E.A. (1969) *Leadership Opinion Questionnaire Manual*, Henley-on-Thames: Science Research Associates.

Fleishman, E.A., Harris, E.F. and Burtt, H.E. (1955) *Leadership and Supervision in Industry*, Columbus: Ohio State University, Bureau of Educational Research.

French, J.R.P. and Raven, B. (1959) 'The bases of power', in D. Cartwright (ed.) *Studies in Social Power*, Ann Arbor: University of Michigan, Institute for Social Research, pp. 150–167.

Fuchs Epstein, C. (1991) 'Ways men and women lead', *Harvard Business Review*, 69(1), 150–151.

Grant, J. (1988) 'Women as managers: What they can offer to organizations', *Organizational Dynamics*, Winter, 56–63.

Green, S. and Mitchell, T.R. (1979) 'Attributional processes of leaders in leader-member interactions', *Organizational Behaviour and Human Performance*, 23, 429–458.

Green, S.G. and Liden, R.C. (1980) 'Contexual and attributional influences on control decisions', *Journal of Applied Psychology*, 65, 453–458.

Greenberg, J. and Baron, R.A. (1993) *Behavior in Organizations* (4th edition), Massachusetts: Allyn & Bacon.

Greene, C.N. (1975) 'The reciprocal nature of influence between leader and subordinate', *Academy of Management Journal*, 20, 32–46.

Greene, C.N. (1979) 'Questions of causation in the path–goal theory of leadership', *Academy of Management Journal*, 22, 22–41.

Greene, C.N. and Podsakoff, P.M. (1981) 'Effects of withdrawal of a performance-contingent reward on supervisory influence and power', *Academy of Management Journal*, 24, 527–542.

Hall, E.T. (1959) *The Silent Language*, New York: Anchor Press/Doubleday.

Hall, E.T. (1976) *Beyond Culture*, New York: Anchor Press/Doubleday.

Hall, E.T. (1983) *The Dance of Life*, New York: Doubleday.

Hall, E.T. and Hall, M.R. (1990) *Understanding Cultural Differences*, Yarmouth, Mass.: Intercultural Press, Inc.

Halpin, A.W. (1957) 'The observed leader behavior and ideal leader behavior of aircraft commanders and school superintendants', in R.M. Stogdill and A.E. Coons (eds) *Leader Behavior: Its Description and Measurement*, Columbus: Ohio State University, Bureau of Business Research.

Handy, C. (1993) *Understanding Organizations*, London: Penguin.

Handy, C. (1994) *The Empty Raincoat: Making sense of the future*, London: Hutchinson.

Heider, F. (1958) *The Psychology of Interpersonal Relations*, New York: John Wiley & Sons.

Heilman, M.E., Hornstein, H.A., Cage, J.H. and Herschlag, J.K. (1984) 'Reactions to prescribed leader behavior as a function of the role perceived: The case of the Vroom–Yetton model', *Journal of Applied Psychology*, 69, 50–60.

Hellriegel, D., Slocum, J.W. and Woodman, R.W. (1992) *Organizational Behavior*, St Paul, Minn.: West Publishing Co.

Hersey, P. and Blanchard, K.H. (1988) *Management of Organizational Behavior* (5th edition), Englewood Cliffs, N.J.: Prentice-Hall.

Hinkin, T.R. and Schriesheim, C.A. (1989) 'Development and application of new scales to measure French and Raven (1959) bases of social power', *Journal of Applied Psychology*, 74, 561–567.

Hofstede, G. (1980) *Culture's Consequences: International Differences in Work-Related Values*, Beverly Hills, Calif.: Sage Publications.

Hofstede, G. (1985) 'The interaction between national and organizational value systems', *Journal of Management Studies*, 22(4), 347–357.

Hofstede, G. (1991) *Cultures and Organizations*, Maidenhead: McGraw-Hill.

Holton, V., Rabbetts, J. and Scrivener, S. (1993) 'Women on the boards of Britain's top 200 companies: A progress report', Ashridge Management Research Group, Ashridge Management College, Berkhamsted, Herts.

House, R.J. (1977) 'A 1976 theory of charismatic leadership', in J.G. Hunt and L.L. Larson (eds) *Leadership: The cutting edge*, Carbondale, Ill.: Southern Illinois University Press, pp. 189–207.

House, R.J. and Mitchell, T.R. (1974) 'Path–goal theory of leadership', *Journal of Contemporary Business*, 3, 81–97.

House, R.J. and Baetz, M.L. (1979) 'Leadership: Some empirical generalizations and new research directions', in B.M. Straw (ed.) *Research in Organizational Behavior*, Vol. 1., Greenwich, Conn.: JAI Press.

House, R.J., Spangler, W.D. and Woycke, J. (1991) 'Personality and charisma in the U.S. presidency: A psychological theory of leadership effectiveness', *Administrative Science Quarterly*, 36, 364–396.

Howell, J.M. and Higgins, C.A. (1990) 'Leadership behaviors, influence tactics, and career experiences of champions of technological innovation', *Leadership Quarterly*, 1, 249–264.

Howell, J.P., Dorfman, P.W. and Kerr, S. (1986) 'Moderator variables in leadership research', *Academy of Management Review*, 11(1), 88–102.

Howell, J.P., Bowen, D.E., Dorfman, P.W., Kerr, S. and Podsakoff, P.M. (1990) 'Substitutes for leadership: Effective alternatives to ineffective leadership', *Organizational Dynamics*, Summer, 20–38.

Ilgen, D.R., Mitchell, T.R. and Frederickson, J.W. (1981) 'Poor performers: Supervisors' and subordinates' responses', *Organizational Behaviour and Human Performance*, 27, 386–410.

Indvik, J. (1986) 'Path–goal theory of leadership: a meta-analysis', Paper presented at the Academy of Management Conference, Chicago.

Jayson, S. and Williams, K. (1986) 'Women in management accounting: Moving up – slowly', *Management Accounting*, 67, 20–24, 63–64.

Jones, E.E. and Nisbett, R.E. (1971) *The Actor and the Observer: Divergent Perceptions of the Causes of Behaviour*, Morristown, N.J.: General Learning Press.

Katerberg, R. and Hom, P.W. (1981) 'Effects of within-group and between-groups variation in leadership', *Journal of Applied Psychology*, 66, 218–223.

Keller, R.T. (1989) 'A test of the path–goal theory of leadership with need for clarity as a moderator in research and development organizations', *Journal of Applied Psychology*, 74, 208–212.

Kelley, H.H. (1967) 'Attribution theory in social psychology', in D. Levine (ed.) *Nebraska Symposium on Motivation*, Vol. 15, M. Lincoln: University of Nebraska Press.

Kerr, S. and Jermier, J.M. (1978) 'Substitutes for leadership: Their meaning and measurement', *Organizational Behavior and Human Performance*, 22, 375–403.

Kirkpatrick, S.A. and Locke, E.A. (1991) 'Leadership: do traits matter?', *The Executive*, 5(2), 48–60.

Kirton, M.J. (1984) 'Adaptors and innovators: Why new initiatives get blocked', *Long Range Planning*, 17(1), 137–143.

Kotter, J.P. (1982) 'What effective general managers really do', *Harvard Business Review*, December.

Kotter, J.P. (1990) *A force for change: how leadership differs from management*, New York: Free Press.

Laurent, A. (1983) 'The cultural diversity of western conceptions of management', *International Studies of Management and Organization*, XIII(1–2), 75–96.

Laurent, A. (1986) 'The cross-cultural puzzle of international human resource management', *Human Resource Management*, 25(1), 91–102.

Leeds, C., Kirkbride, P.S. and Durcan, J. (1993) 'The cultural context of Europe: A tentative mapping', in P.S. Kirkbride (ed.) *Human Resource Management in Europe: Perspectives for the 1990s*, London: Routledge.

Locke, E.A. (1991) *The Essence of Leadership: The Four Keys to Leading Successfully*, New York: Lexington.

Loden, M. (1985) *Feminine Leadership or How to Succeed in Business Without Being One of the Boys*, New York: Times Books.

Lombardo, M.M. and Eichinger, R.W. (1989) 'Preventing derailment: What to do before it's too late', Application Report, Center for Creative Leadership, Greensboro, North Carolina.

Lord, R.G., DeVader, C.L. and Alliger, G.M. (1986) 'A meta-analysis of the relation between personality traits and leadership perceptions: An application of validity generalization procedures', *Journal of Applied Psychology*, 71, 402–410.

Margerison, C.J. (1980) 'How chief executives succeed', *Journal of European Industrial Training*, 4(5), 1–32.

Margerison, C. and Glube, R. (1979) 'Leadership decision-making: An empirical test of the Vroom and Yetton model', *Journal of Management Studies*, 16, 45–55.

McCall, M.W. and Lombardo, M.M. (1983) *Off the Track: Why and How Successful Executives Get Derailed*, Center for Creative Leadership, Greensboro, Report No. 21.

McClelland, D.C. (1971) 'The two faces of power', in D.A. Colb, I.M. Rubin and J.M. McIntyre, *Organizational Psychology* (2nd edition), Englewood Cliffs, N.J.: Prentice-Hall.

McClelland, D.C. (1985) *Human Motivation*, Glenview, Ill.: Scott, Foresman.

McClelland, D.C. and Burnham, D.H. (1976) 'Power is the Great Motivator',

Harvard Business Review, vol. 54, 100–101.

McLoughlin, C.S., Friedson, W.S. and Murray, J.N. (1983) 'Personality profiles of recently terminated executives', *Personnel and Guidance Journal*, 61, 226–229.

Meindl, J.R. (1989) 'On leadership: An alternative to conventional wisdom', Paper presented at the Fourth International Conference on Organizational Symbolism and Corporate Culture, INSEAD.

Meindl, J.R. (1992) 'Reinventing leadership: A radical, social psychological approach', in Keith Murnigham (ed.) *Social Psychology in Organizations: Advances in Theory and Research*, Englewood Cliffs, N.J.: Prentice-Hall.

Meindl, J.R. and Ehrlich, S.B. (1987) 'The romance of leadership and the evaluation of organizational performance', *Academy of Management Journal*, 30(1), 91–109.

Meindl, J.R., Ehrlich, S.B. and Dukerich, J.M. (1985) 'The romance of leadership', *Administrative Science Quarterly*, 30, 78–102.

Milgram, S. (1963) 'Behavioural study of obedience', *Journal of Abnormal Psychology*, 67, 371–378.

Milgram, S. (1974) *Obedience to Authority: An Experimental View*, New York: Harper & Row.

Mischel, W. (1973) 'Towards a cognitive social learning reconceptualization of personality', *Psychological Review*, 80, 252–283.

Mitchell, T.R. (1973) 'Motivation and participation: An integration', *Academy of Management Journal*, June, 160–179.

Mitchell, T.R. (1979) 'Organizational Behaviour Annual Review of Psychology', Palo Alto, Calif.: Annual Reviews, 30, 243–282.

Mitchell, T.R. and Wood, R.E. (1979) 'An empirical test of an attributional model of leader's responses to poor performance', *Academy of Management Proceedings*, in Richard C. Huseman (ed.) Starksville, Miss.: Academy of Management.

Mitchell, T.R. and Wood, R.E. (1980) 'Supervisors' responses to subordinate poor performance: A test of an attributional model', *Organizational Behaviour and Human Performance*, 25, 123–138.

Moorhead, G. and Griffin, R.W. (1992) *Organizational Behaviour* (3rd edition), Boston, Mass.: Houghton Mifflin Co.

Morrison, A.M., White, R.P. and Van Velsor, E. (1986) 'The glass house dilemma: Why women executives dare not fail', *Working Women*, October, 110–112.

Morrison, A.M., White, R.P. and Van Velsor, E. (1987) *Breaking the Glass Ceiling*, Reading, Mass.: Addison-Wesley.

Muczyk, J.P. and Reimann, B.C. (1987) 'The case for directive leadership', *Academy of Management Review*, 12, 637–647.

Mulder, M. (1977) *The Daily Power Game*, Leiden: Martinus Nijhoff.

Newell, S. (1995, in press) *The Healthy Organization*, London: Routledge.

Nicholson, N. and West, M.A. (1988) *Managerial Job Change: Men and Women in Transition*, Cambridge: Cambridge University Press.

Nisbett, R.E. and Ross, L. (1985) *Human Inference: Strategies and Short-comings of Social Judgement* (reprint edition), Englewood Cliffs, N.J.: Prentice-Hall.

Peters, T.J. and Waterman, R.H. (1982) *In Search of Excellence*, New York: Harper & Row.

Peters, L.H., Hartke, D.D. and Pohlmann, J.T. (1985) 'Fiedler's contingency theory of leadership: An application of the meta-analysis procedures of Schmidt and Huner', *Psychological Bulletin*, 97, 224–285.

Pillai, R. and Meindl, J.R. (1991) 'The impact of a performance crisis on attributions of charismatic leadership: A preliminary study', *Best Paper Proceedings of the 1991 Eastern Academy of Management Meetings*, Hartford, Conn.

Plant, R. (1987) *Managing Change and Making it Stick*, London: Fontana.

Podsakoff, P.M. and Schriesheim, C.A. (1985) 'Field studies of French and Raven's bases of power: Critique, reanalysis and suggestions for future research', *Psychological Bulletin*, 97(3), 387–411.

Podsakoff, P.M., Dorfman, P.W., Howell, J.P. and Todor, W.D. (1986) 'Leader reward and punishment behaviours: A preliminary test of a culture-free style of leadership effectiveness', in R.N. Farmer (ed.) *Advances in International Comparative Management*, Vol. 2, Greenwich, Conn.: JAI Press, pp. 95–138.

Podsakoff, P.M., MacKenzie, S.B., Morrman, R.H. and Fetter, R. (1990) 'Transformational leader behaviors and their effects on follower's trust in leader, satisfaction, and organizational citizenship behaviors', *Leadership Quarterly*, 1, 107–142.

Puffer, S.M. (1990) 'Attributions of charismatic leadership: the impact of decision style, outcome, and observer characteristics', *Leadership Quarterly*, 1, 177–192.

Rahim, A. (1981) 'Organizational behaviour course for graduate students in business administration: Views from the tower and the battlefield', *Psychological Reports*, 49, 583–592.

Reddin, W.J. (1970) *Managerial Effectiveness*, New York: McGraw-Hill.

Roddick, A. (1991) *Body and Soul*, London: Ebury Press.

Rosener, J.B. (1990) 'Ways women lead', *Harvard Business Review*, 68(6), 119–125.

Ross, L. (1977) 'The intuitive psychologist and his shortcomings: Distortion in the attribution process', in L. Berkowitz (ed.) *Advances in Experimental Social Psychology*, Vol. 10, New York: Academic Press.

Sadler, P.J. (1970) 'Leadership style, confidence in management, and job satisfaction', *The Journal of Applied Behavioral Science*, 6(1), 3–19.

Sadler, P. (1993) *Managing Talent: Making the Best of the Best*, London: Century Business.

Schein, V.E. (1973) 'The relationship between sex role stereotypes and requisite management characteristics', *Journal of Applied Psychology*, 57, 95–100.

Schein, V.E. (1975) 'Relationships between sex role stereotypes and requisite management characteristics among female managers', *Journal of Applied Psychology*, 60, 340–344.

Schriesheim, C.A. and Murphy, C.J. (1976) 'Relationships between leader behavior and subordinate satisfaction and performance: a test of some situational moderators', *Journal of Applied Psychology*, 61, 634–641.

Schriesheim, J.F. and Schriesheim, C.A. (1980) 'A test of the path–goal theory of leadership and some suggested directions for future research', *Personnel Psychology*, 33, 349–370.

Schriesheim, C.A. and DeNisi, A.S. (1981) 'Task dimensions of the effects of instrumental leadership: A two-sample replicated test of path–goal leadership theory', *Journal of Applied Psychology*, 66, 589–597.

Shackleton, V.J. (1992) 'Using a competency approach in a business change setting', in R. Boam and P. Sparrow (eds) *Designing and Achieving Competency: A Competency Based Approach to Developing People and Organizations*, London: McGraw-Hill.

Shamir, B. (1991) 'Meaning, self and motivation in organizations', *Organization Studies*, 12, 405–424.

Shamir, B., House, R.J. and Arthur, M.B. (1993) 'The motivational effects of charismatic leadership: A self-concept based theory', *Organization Science*, 4, 1–17.

Sheridan, J.E., Vredenburgh, D.J. and Abelson, M.A. (1984) 'Contextual model of leadership influence in hospital units', *Academy of Management Journal*, 27(1), 57–78.

Smith, P.B. and Bond, M.H. (1993) *Social Psychology Across Cultures: Analysis and Perspectives*, Herts, England: Harvester Wheatsheaf.

Smith, P.B., Misumi, J., Tayeb, M., Peterson, M. and Bond, M. (1989) 'On the generality of leadership style measures across cultures', *Journal of Occupational Psychology*, 62, 97–109.

Stoeberl, P.A. and Schneiderjans, M.J. (1981) 'The ineffective subordinate: A management survey', *Personnel Administrator*, 26(2), 72–76.

Stogdill, R. (1974) *Handbook of Leadership*, New York: Free Press.

Strube, M.J. and Garcia, J.E. (1981) 'A meta-analytic investigation of Fiedler's contingency model of leadership effectiveness', *Psychological Bulletin*, 90, 307–321.

Tang, S.F. and Kirkbride, P.S. (1986) 'Developing conflict management skills in Hong Kong: An analysis of some cross-cultural implications', Special Issue, International Management and Development Management, *Management Education and Development*, 17(3), 287–301.

Tannenbaum, R. and Schmidt, W.H. (1958) 'How to choose a leadership pattern', *Harvard Business Review*, 36(2), 95–101.

Terkel, S. (1974) *Working*, New York: Pantheon.

Tichy, N.M. and Devanna, M.A. (1986) *The Transformational Leader*, New York: Wiley.

Tjosvold, D., Wedley, W.C. and Field, R.H.G. (1986) 'Constructive controversy, the Vroom–Yetton model, and managerial decision-making', *Journal of Occupational Behaviour*, 7, 125–138.

Trice, H.M. and Beyer, J.M. (1991) 'Cultural leadership in organizations', *Organizational Science*, 2, 149–169.

Trompenaars, F. (1993) *Riding the Waves of Culture: Understanding Cultural Diversity in Business*, London: Nicholas Brealey Publishing.

Turban, D.B., Jones, A.P. and Rozelle, R.M. (1990) 'Influences of supervisor liking of a subordinate and the reward context on the treatment and evaluation of that subordinate', *Motivation and Emotion*, 14(3), 215–233.

Tyson, S., Barclay, C. and Handyside, J. (1986) *The 'N' Factor in Executive Survival*, Cranfield: Cranfield Press.

Vecchio, R.P. (1987) 'Situational leadership theory: An examination of a prescriptive theory', *Journal of Applied Psychology*, 72, 444–451.

Vecchio, R.P. (1991) *Organizational Behaviour* (2nd edition), Orlando, Fla.: Harcourt Brace Jovanovich Inc., The Dryden Press, Saunders College Publishers.

Vroom, V.H. (1984) 'Reflections on leadership and decision-making', *Journal of General Management*, 9, 18–36.

Vroom, V.H. and Yetton, P.W. (1973) *Leadership and Decision Making*, Pittsburg, Pa.: University of Pittsburg Press.

Vroom, V.H. and Jago, A.G. (1978) 'On the validity of the Vroom–Yetton model', *Journal of Applied Psychology*, 63, 151–162.

Vroom, V.H. and Jago, A.G. (1988) *The New Leadership: Managing Participation in Organizations*, Englewood Cliffs, N.J.: Prentice-Hall.

Westwood, R.I., Tang, S.F. and Kirkbride, P.S. (1992) 'Chinese conflict behaviour: Cultural antecedents and behavioural consequences', *Organization Development Journal*, 10(2), 13–19.

Williams, M.L., Podsakoff, P.M., Lodor, W.S., Huber, V.L., Howell, J.P. and Dorfman, P.W. (1988) 'A preliminary analysis of the construct validity of Kerr & Jermier's substitutes for leadership scales', *Journal of Occupational Psychology*, 61, 307–333.

Willner, A.R. (1984) *The Spellbinders: Charismatic Political Leadership*, New Haven: Yale University Press.

Wilson, D. (1992) *A Strategy of Change: Concepts and Controversies in the Management of Change*, London: Routledge.

Wood, R.E. and Mitchell, T.R. (1981) 'Manager behaviour in a social context: The impact of impression management on attributions and disciplinary actions', *Organizational Behaviour and Human Performance*, 28, 356–378.

Yammarino, F.J. and Bass, B.M. (1990) 'Transformational leadership and multiple levels of analysis', *Human Relations*, 43, 975–995.

Yukl, G.A. (1989) *Leadership in Organizations* (2nd edition), New York: Academic Press.

Yukl, G.A. (1994) *Leadership in Organizations* (3rd edition), Englewood Cliffs, N.J.: Prentice-Hall.

Yukl, G.A. and Taber, T. (1983) 'The effective use of managerial power', *Personnel*, March–April, 37–44.

Yukl, G.A. and Falbe, C.M. (1990) 'Influence tactics and objectives in upward, downward and lateral influence attempts', *Journal of Applied Psychology*, 75, 132–140.

Yukl, G.A. and Falbe, C.M. (1991) 'Importance of different power sources in downward and lateral relations', *Journal of Applied Psychology*, 76, 416–423.

Zajonc, R.B. (1980) 'Feeling and thinking: Preferences need no inferences', *American Psychologist*, 35, 151–175.

— *Index*

Note: Numbers in *italic* refer to pages with tables; numbers in **bold** refer to main references.